Shropshire
MURDERS

NICOLA SLY

The History Press

ALSO BY THE AUTHOR

Bristol Murders
Cornish Murders (with John Van der Kiste)
Dorset Murders
Hampshire Murders
Somerset Murders (with John Van der Kiste)
Wiltshire Murders

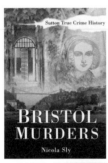
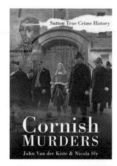

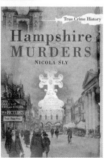
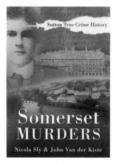
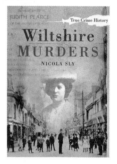

First published 2009

The History Press
The Mill, Brimscombe Port
Stroud, Gloucestershire, GL5 2QG
www.thehistorypress.co.uk

© Nicola Sly, 2009

The right of Nicola Sly to be identified as the Author
of this work has been asserted in accordance with the
Copyrights, Designs and Patents Act 1988.

British Library Cataloguing in Publication Data.
A catalogue record for this book is available from the British Library.

ISBN 978 0 7524 4897 8

Typesetting and origination by The History Press
Printed in Great Britain

CONTENTS

AUTHOR'S NOTE & ACKNOWLEDGEMENTS

I was delighted to be asked to compile *Shropshire Murders*, since I have family living in the area and have always enjoyed exploring the county's beautiful countryside and its historic towns with their timbered buildings and narrow winding streets. My enthusiasm waned slightly when my initial research seemed to show that, historically, Shropshire had case after case of 'Attempted Murder'. (These included my relatives' neighbour, a habitual drunkard, who determined to murder his wife. Fortunately for her, he was so befuddled by drink at the time that he actually shot her reflection in the mirror!) However, as this collection of true cases demonstrates, in every county there are always some people who, for one reason or another, are prepared to take a human life.

Several of the cases involve the murders of children, such as those of Edward Cooper, who murdered his son in Baschurch in 1862; John Mapp of Longden, who brutally murdered nine-year-old Catherine Lewis in 1867; and Desmond Hooper, who killed twelve-year-old Betty Smith near Atcham in 1953. Murders by jealous husbands and boyfriends account for several more, including the murder of Eliza Bowen by Richard Wigley at Westbury in 1901. Some of the killers were judged to be insane at the time of their crimes, while others claimed inebriation as the reason why they murdered, such as George Riley who killed elderly widow, Adeline Smith, at Shrewsbury in 1960, while trying to steal her handbag.

As always, there are numerous people to be acknowledged and thanked. John J. Eddleston, George Glover, Paul Harrison and Anthony Hunt have all previously published books either on murder in Shropshire or more general reference works on British murders and executions. These books are recorded in more detail in the bibliography, as are the local and national newspapers from which the details of the featured cases were drawn. My thanks must also go to the staff of the Shropshire Archives for their help with my research.

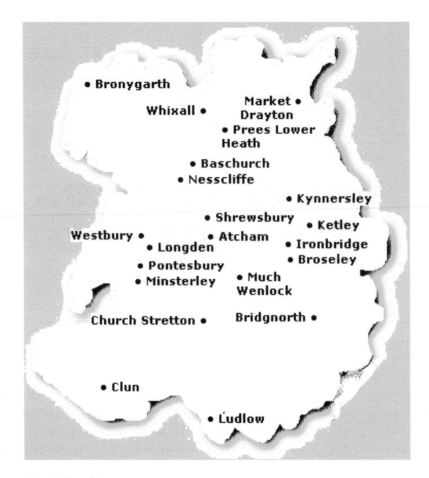

Map of Shropshire.

I am especially grateful to the Thomas Porter Blunt website (http://members.shaw.ca/TPBlunt/index.htm) for allowing me to use their photograph on page 72 and for providing me with some fascinating information about the Blunt family history. Analysts Thomas Porter Blunt and his father, Thomas W. Blunt, appear in two chapters and, in both cases, their work was a vital part of the police investigations.

On a more personal level, John Van der Kiste was, as always, generous with his help and support. My long-suffering husband, Richard, proof read every word of the book and made invaluable suggestions on how each chapter could be improved. He also acted as chauffeur for the research and photography trips from Cornwall to Shropshire and even took the occasional photograph himself. My grateful thanks also go to my brother-in-law and sister-in-law, John and Sue, who opened their home to us during our research trip to Shropshire. My father, John Higginson, was as supportive and encouraging as ever.

Finally, my thanks must go to Matilda Richards, my editor at The History Press, for her continued help and encouragement.

1

'OH, DEAR, DAD, DO NOT!'

On 21 January 1823, tinsmith and brazier George Edwards paid a visit to John Newton at his farm at Severn Hall, near Bridgnorth. The purpose of Edwards' visit was to collect his outstanding account from the farmer and, as was customary on these occasions, he was invited into the farmhouse and given a drink of beer, while Newton closely scrutinised the bill before paying it.

On this occasion, Newton paused in his examination of the bill querying the inclusion of a lamp, which had cost 3*s*. Newton insisted that he had given his wife, Sarah, the money to pay for the lamp and was most displeased to see that it had not been paid for. In a passion, Newton called for his wife, who came into the room. He asked her if he had given her the money to pay for the lamp and Sarah had to agree that he had.

This was enough to send John Newton into a rage. Telling the embarrassed Edwards that Sarah was always running him into debt, he promised to give her a good thrashing. Edwards advised him not to do so, saying that he would rather strike the lamp off the bill than have it cause an argument.

Edwards left the farm at about eight o'clock in the evening, passing through the kitchen on his way out. Sarah, who was five months pregnant, was sitting by the fire, looking upset. Edwards paused for long enough to shake hands with her and tell her to keep her spirits up then he walked into the yard, accompanied by John Newton. Before leaving, Edwards called out 'Good night' to Sarah, but there was no reply.

'Oh, she's gone to hide herself; she knows what to expect.' Newton told him.

Edwards again warned Newton about beating his wife, threatening never to speak to him again if he harmed her. He then took his leave of John Newton and returned home to Bridgnorth.

In the early hours of the morning, Edwards was awakened by knocking on his door. When he went to answer it, he was surprised to find John Newton on his doorstep.

'A bad job has happened,' explained Newton, telling Edwards that Sarah was very ill.

'Good God, Mr Newton, I hope you have done nothing wrong,' responded Edwards, but Newton told him that he hadn't struck his wife but that a complication had arisen in her pregnancy. He asked to be directed to the home of Dr Hall and Edwards pointed out the surgeon's house then returned to his bed.

Earlier, a servant at the farm had been sent on a lengthy errand, which involved crossing the River Severn. Mary Jones left the farm at about four o'clock in the afternoon and returned at about eight o'clock. As she crossed the fields on her route home, she was four fields away from the farm when she heard the terrible sounds of children screaming, 'Oh, dear, Dad, do not!'

Mary picked up her skirts and ran, continuing to hear the children shouting and crying in fear as she neared the house. As she entered, she found Sarah Newton lying on the floor by the front door, her eight-year-old son, John, by her side, trying his best to comfort her. Noticing that her mistress's lower garments were soaked with blood, Mary called for help and soon John Newton arrived. He roused two more servants, Julia Oliver and William Batch, from their beds, telling them to get up and care for their mistress. Newton then left the house to summon Sarah Lloyd, a widow from Bridgnorth who was frequently called upon to attend the sick. Mrs Lloyd accompanied Newton back to the farm and found Sarah Newton lying on her side by the hearth in a pool of blood, her knees pulled up to her stomach. She had a black eye and a cut lip. Mrs Lloyd asked the farmer's wife who had done this to her, but Sarah did not reply. In fact, the only time Sarah had spoken properly was when she called servant William Batch to her side and told him, 'God bless you, Will. I take my leave of you.'

Sarah Newton was put to bed with Mrs Lloyd in attendance. Meanwhile John Newton also went to bed, after first asking Mary Jones about his wife's condition. She told him that her mistress was very ill, to which Newton replied, 'She must thank herself for that, for having bills brought in.' Mary then suggested that Newton went to fetch a doctor, but Newton said that he couldn't go, so Mary said she would go herself. Eventually, William Batch was sent for Dr Hall, who was out when he arrived at his home.

His assistant, Mr Barber, came to the farm in Hall's stead. He examined Sarah Newton briefly and believed her to be 'in great danger'. Nevertheless, the only treatment he prescribed was for Mary Jones to put vinegar and water on the cuts and bruises and to give her mistress a dose of laudanum and brandy. He then left.

Mary Jones roused John Newton at just after midnight to inform him that his wife had died. Newton seemed disbelieving, telling Mary that he was sure that Sarah had just fainted or fallen into a fit. When Mary finally managed to convince him that she was telling the truth, Newton jumped out of bed and announced his intention of going to fetch a doctor.

Between one and two o'clock in the morning, he arrived at Mr Hall's, asking for a doctor to attend his wife, whom he believed was dying. Hall was still out and Barber told Newton that he believed he had done all he could for his wife. He gave him a bottle of medicine and sent Newton home, refusing to go back to the farm with him. The next time Barber saw Sarah Newton it was in the company of Dr Hall, at her post-mortem examination, which was carried out by Mr James Milman Coley. The doctors determined that Sarah Newton had bled to death following what they described as 'external violence'.

John Newton appeared distraught at his wife's death, telling William Batch that he 'would give all the world for her again.' He also admitted to Batch that he had hit Sarah two or three times with his hand, but insisted that the blows had not been hard ones and certainly not sufficient to cause her death. Before the inquest into his wife's death took place, Newton instructed Mary Jones that she was not to say that she had heard the children screaming when still four fields away from the house. However, Mary Jones disobeyed him and told the truth, which infuriated Newton.

The coroner's jury found that Sarah Newton had 'died by bleeding, the cause of which is unknown to us.' The police found themselves under pressure, particularly from Sarah's brother, to charge John Newton with Sarah's murder, and eventually Newton was committed to stand trial for wilful murder at the next Shropshire Assizes. His trial opened on 22 March 1823, before Mr Justice Best.

At the trial, tinsmith George Edwards was called to give evidence first, and was followed into the dock by servants Mary Jones, Julia Oliver and William Batch then Mrs Lloyd and Ann Jones, the mother of servant, Mary. It was then the turn of Mr James Barber, the assistant to surgeon Mr Hall.

Barber was heavily criticised by the judge for leaving Sarah Newton in so serious a condition and for not returning to the farm when he was called to do so. It was suggested that Barber should have made more effort to determine the source of Sarah Newton's bleeding and to stop the blood loss. However, Barber insisted that, by the time he attended Mrs Newton, she had already lost a great deal of blood and her pulse had dropped to below thirty beats per minute. Telling the court that he had nine years experience as a medical assistant, he insisted that giving a dose of laudanum was the most appropriate treatment. Still, one doctor, Mr Ebenezer Vaughan, believed that Sarah Newton could have been saved, had the right medical treatment been given.

The medical witnesses all agreed that Sarah Newton had died as a result of blood loss and, since the newspapers of the time seemed strangely reluctant to detail her injuries, it can probably be assumed that she had a miscarriage, caused by the beating and kicking she had been given by her husband.

In Newton's defence, it was pointed out that she had once before haemorrhaged after giving birth. The doctors were questioned as to whether or not Sarah could have worked herself up into a temper, causing her blood vessels to rupture, but they assured the court that this was not the case. Neither was it believed that 'hard labour' could have occasioned her death. In his own defence, John Newton told the court that he had been drunk at the time and that his wife had started the fight by attacking him – he had hit her only in self defence and had never meant to do her any harm. After that, the counsel for the defence called a number of witnesses in an attempt to prove to the court that John Newton had been insane at the time of the murder.

The first of these was Mr John Hewit, who was employed as an apothecary at Shrewsbury Gaol, where Newton had been confined since his arrest. Hewit testified that Newton had originally been 'labouring under a great dejection of spirits' on his admission to prison. However, on the third day of his incarceration, Newton had suddenly become incoherent and violent and Hewit had been forced to have him manacled in order to control him. He had remained in this manic state for two days before the medicines prescribed by Hewit finally took effect and made him calmer and quieter.

Under cross-examination, Hewit told the court that, although he had read a book on diseases in general, he had never read anything specific on diseases of the mind, neither had he ever been in charge of an insane prisoner. Even so, he continued to insist that Newton was insane.

Several witnesses then testified to a history of insanity in Newton's family. His brother, James, had been an inmate in Stafford Asylum. Newton's uncle told the court that both Newton's mother's uncle and cousin had died insane, while her sister had also spent time as an inmate in an asylum. In response to a direct question from the judge, the uncle stated that he had never known the accused to be insane.

However, other people disagreed. An employee of Newton's father, with whom Newton had shared a bed, spoke of Newton discharging a gun in the bedroom for no apparent reason and having been found several times wandering stark naked in the farmyard during the night. John Taylor firmly believed that John Newton was 'affected in his head' and had even told Newton's mother that he believed this to be the case.

Mr Coley, who was once the Newton's family physician, stated that he had attended John Newton regularly and had never seen him display the slightest sign of insanity. Mr Hall, who had taken over from Coley as the Newton's doctor, had treated John less frequently but agreed with his colleague that he was perfectly sane.

The judge then recalled George Edwards to question him on the amount of beer that had been consumed during the afternoon before Sarah Newton's death. Edwards stated that five or six jugs of beer had been shared between three people, but that it had been very weak. He had been sober when he left the Newton's farm and he believed the same could be said of the defendant.

There had been some discussion in court as to whether or not to call the Newton's children to give evidence, particularly John, the oldest child. However, the judge gave his opinion that young John could add little to the proceedings and it would be extremely distressing for him to testify, hence it was decided not to involve him.

Thus it only remained for the judge to summarise the case for the benefit of the jury. He told them that they must first decide whether or not the deceased came to her death by an act of the accused. Secondly, if they believed that Sarah Newton had died as a result of a violent act committed by the accused, was her death murder or manslaughter? And thirdly, was the accused in a state of mind to know what he was doing and to understand the difference between good and evil.

On the first point, the judge conceded that there had been some argument between the medical witnesses but that all of them had concurred that a kick given to a woman in Sarah Newton's situation would probably cause death. Addressing the question of murder or manslaughter, the judge pointed out that no weapon had been used, but if John Newton had beaten his wife to death when there was no evidence of immediate prior provocation then he would be guilty of murder. Finally, with regard to the defendant's state of mind at the time of the attack, the judge said that being a wayward or passionate man was not sufficient to excuse the defendant, nor would it be sufficient to suggest a defence on the grounds of insanity. If a lunatic had lucid intervals, during which he committed a crime, then he would still be liable to suffer the full penalties of the law. If the jury believed that John Newton was insane they should acquit him on those grounds. However, if they believed that he was sane and that he had committed a considered act of violence that had caused the death of his wife then they should do their duty to their country and find him guilty.

The jury deliberated for only two or three minutes before finding John Newton 'Guilty of the wilful murder of his wife, Sarah'.

The judge pronounced the prescribed death sentence on a bewildered looking John Newton, who looked around him as if expecting something else to happen. Only when the warders began to remove him from the dock did he begin to react to his sentence, fighting and struggling and begging the court not to kill him. It took considerable force to remove him from court and, for some minutes after his departure, his desperate cries and entreaties for mercy continued to echo through the courtroom.

Forty-year-old Newton was executed at Shrewsbury on 24 March 1823. However, his death was not the final episode in the case of Sarah Newton as, in June 1823, Mr Whitcombe, the coroner who had conducted her inquest, was charged with malpractice.

It was alleged that, on arriving at the farm to conduct the proceedings, he had a private interview with John Newton and that this had swayed his judgement. Whitcombe had not arranged for George Edwards to attend the inquest, even though he was a material witness, who was alluded to many times during the proceedings.

Furthermore, he had allowed improper interference from a magistrate, Mr Whitmore, who was also John Newton's landlord. He had refused to allow the jury to inspect Sarah Newton's body and had also dismissed half the jury because he considered the case to be trifling. Finally, he had induced the jury to find a 'nugatory verdict' after first having attempted to persuade them to find that death had occurred 'by visitation of God.'

Whitcombe offered an explanation for all the charges against him. His interview with Newton had been accidental – he had not known him and had exchanged a few remarks with him in passing. Edwards had never been proposed to him as a witness and, with regard to Mr Whitmore, Whitcombe believed that the man's experience and local knowledge were highly valuable to the proceedings and had therefore allowed him to participate in the inquest.

The jury had viewed the body, but only after the post-mortem examination, when it was covered by a sheet, so that only the face was visible. Any member of the jury could have lifted the sheet had he so desired, but the coroner had not insisted that they viewed the body in its entirety in order to spare their feelings.

Whitcombe had dismissed twelve members of the jury, but had not done so until Mr Coley had stated that it was impossible to determine the cause of the bleeding. It had been a cold, wet day and, after consulting with Mr Whitmore, the coroner had thought it futile to keep jury members away from their homes. Finally, Whitcombe denied trying to influence the jury in any way.

At a preliminary hearing, it was decided that Whitcombe should stand trial at the next county assizes, charged with attempting to pervert the course of justice for his own private gain. The trial took place in July 1823, with Mr Baron Hullock presiding.

All the witnesses who had attended the original inquest were reassembled to testify, including Mr Coley, the surgeon who had inspected the body at the inquest in the presence of the coroner. He stated that Whitcombe's inspection of the body was only perfunctory and that the coroner seemed to have already formed the unshakeable opinion that the deceased died from 'flooding', contrary to Mr Coley's own opinion. Whitcombe had also suggested several times that Sarah Newton's injuries might have resulted from a fall over a stile, the implication being that this explanation had been offered to him by John Newton, with whom he certainly had a private interview prior to the start of the inquest.

Whitcombe had made a grave error of judgement in allowing Mrs Newton's body to be dissected before it had been inspected by the jury and had been unwise in allowing Mr Whitmore to play such a large part in the proceedings, given that Whitmore had a long association with the Newton family, which was described as 'almost familial.'

The jury at Whitcombe's trial found him 'Guilty of a gross violation of his duty', although they added a rider to say that they had found no evidence that he had accepted a bribe. In view of the fact that Whitcombe had now retired from his post as coroner he escaped punishment for his transgressions.

2

'I HAVE THE TRUTH AT MY TONGUE'S END, BUT I DARE NOT SPEAK IT'

Bridgnorth, 1823

On 21 September 1823, Jonathan and Louisa Davies were enjoying a quiet Sunday morning at home in Bridgnorth, when the peace was suddenly shattered by the sound of a woman's piercing screams coming from the cottage adjoining theirs. Louisa immediately went next door to see if she could help.

She found several people at the house, including Richard Overfield and his wife, who was clutching her three-month-old baby boy to her breast. The baby, named Richard after his father, appeared to be in agony and was struggling so violently that Mrs Overfield was having difficulty keeping him on her lap. As Louisa Davies watched, Mrs Overfield bent over and slipped her tongue into the baby's mouth, saying that there was some bitter-tasting substance there that was making her own mouth smart.

'Dick, what have you done to my child?' she asked her husband, to which Richard Overfield nonchalantly replied that he had done nothing to harm it. In fact, quite the contrary – he had actually just rescued the baby, as, having come into the room and found a black cat sucking the infant's breath away, he had knocked the cat off the child.

Mrs Overfield scooped up her baby and ran with him to the home of Mr Hall, the Bridgnorth surgeon. She arrived so distressed and out of breath that, for a few moments, she was unable to tell Hall's assistant Mr Edward Spry the purpose of her visit.

BRIDGNORTH FROM CASTLE HILL.

Bridgnorth in 1927. (Author's collection)

Eventually, she pointed to her son's mouth and told Mr Spry to taste it, which he did, finding it to have a pungent, acidic taste.

When he examined the baby, Spry found that its lips were white and rather shrivelled, with small blisters on the inside of the mouth and the tongue. He concluded that the baby had somehow swallowed acid and, from its taste, he identified the substance as sulphuric acid, otherwise known as oil of vitriol.

Realising the seriousness of the child's condition, he immediately called for Mr Hall and the two doctors agreed that the best course of treatment was magnesia in water to neutralise the acid, followed by alternating drinks of diluted gruel and barley water.

Mrs Overfield left with the baby and Mr Spry followed her home almost immediately. When he reached her house, he found the room full of neighbours, one of whom had the child on her lap and was struggling to administer the magnesia he had just prescribed. Spry began to question Richard Overfield about what had happened, asking him if he had given the baby any food or medicine, either deliberately or by mistake. Overfield denied giving the baby anything at all, insisting that all he had done was to knock the cat off the baby.

'Where is the cat now?' asked Spry. Overfield replied that it had gone out. Spry asked a neighbour to go out and find the animal and was soon presented with a black cat, which Overfield assured him was the one that had been sucking away the baby's breath. Spry examined the animal, thoroughly checking its paws and coat and finding nothing unusual. He inserted his little finger into the cat's mouth then tasted it, but could detect no trace of the acid that he had tasted on the child.

Spry then informed Overfield that he believed the baby had been given oil of vitriol and asked him if there was any in the house. Overfield told him that there wasn't and denied even knowing what oil of vitriol was. Spry explained some of the common household uses of oil of vitriol, such as cleaning brass and making blacking, but Overfield continued to deny ever having heard of it.

Next Spry examined the baby again, paying particular attention to its clothes. The child's frock was made from dyed cotton, which, Spry knew, would turn red when it came into contact with acid. There were two or three small red spots on the front of the garment and, when Spry touched his tongue to them, he tasted the same bitter taste. There was a similar spot on the front of Mrs Overfield's dress, where the child's lips had apparently made contact with the material there, but no red spots on her husband's clothing.

By now, the child's condition was obviously deteriorating rapidly and Spry went back to fetch Mr Hall. By the time Hall returned, the child was foaming at the mouth and seemed incapable of swallowing. He weakened gradually until, at three o'clock that afternoon, he finally died.

Mrs Overfield was understandably beside herself with grief and her neighbours took turns staying with her. On the day after the baby's death, she suddenly fainted and, when she was brought round, her neighbour Louisa Davies escorted her into the garden for a breath of fresh air. The end of the garden was fenced off with palings, which divided it from a communal cattle fold, used by many of the local people. As Louisa Davies neared the fence, she happened to glance through a gap in the palings and spotted a small phial on the other side. She reached through the fence and picked it up.

The phial was corked and contained about a teaspoonful of black liquid. When Louisa removed the cork and sniffed the contents, she instantly recoiled from the strong, acidic odour. She immediately contacted the police and, on the arrival of PC Edward Goodall, handed the little bottle into his keeping. Goodall took the bottle straight to Mr Spry and Mr Hall, who removed a few drops of the liquid contents, then gave it back to the policeman. On analysis, the liquid was found to be oil of vitriol.

A post-mortem examination was conducted on the dead infant by Mr Hall, accompanied by Mr Dugard, a physician from Shrewsbury. When the child's body was opened, almost a pint of bloody fluid ran from it, which was collected and retained for testing. It was later shown to be oil of vitriol and was present in sufficient quantity to constitute a fatal dose for the baby. The child's stomach was corroded and blackened, the stomach walls having the consistency of wet brown paper. The gullet was similarly destroyed and the inside of the child's mouth and its tongue were a dull white in colour.

The child had obviously been fed sulphuric acid and the most likely suspect was Richard Overfield. When police interviewed his neighbour on the other side, an elderly woman called Mary Nichols, she told them that, on the morning of 21 September, she had seen Overfield come out of his house and walk down the garden. At the bottom of the garden, he briefly stooped down before getting up and returning to the house. Mary Nichols pointed out to the police the spot where she had seen Overfield bending – it was exactly the same place from which Louisa Davies had retrieved the poison bottle.

Overfield went to work on 22 September. He had been employed for many years as a labourer in a carpet factory, where he washed worsted yarns prior to them being woven into carpets. One of the processes of carpet manufacture required extensive use of oil of vitriol and the factory where Overfield worked used several gallons each week.

Thomas Southwell, Overfield's supervisor at work, approached him on the day after the child's death and demanded to know if reports of a child being poisoned were true.

Overfield said he didn't know.

'Is the child dead?' persisted Southwell.

'Yes', replied Overfield.

'You must have been in the house,' said Southwell, growing exasperated with Overfield's reticence. 'You must know what caused its death?'

Overfield then explained, 'I was standing by the fire doing something to the pot. I heard the child cry and turned myself round, when I saw a black cat sucking its breath. I knocked it off and that is all I know about it.'

Southwell told him that there would be an inquest and the child would be opened. 'Let them open it and then they will see,' replied Overfield.

The results of the post-mortem examination, coupled with the finding of the phial of sulphuric acid and Mary Nichol's statement to the police connecting Overfield with the act of concealing it behind the fence, were sufficient grounds for him to be charged with the murder of his son. Constable Goodall went to Overfield's house on 25 September and arrested him as he returned from work, taking him to the police house at Bridgnorth to await transportation to Shrewsbury Gaol.

While he was there, his wife came to see him, telling him, 'My dear Dick, go down on your knees and pray to the Almighty to forgive you for what you have done. And always have the truth in your mouth.'

'I have the truth at my tongue's end, but I dare not speak it,' replied Overfield then added, 'My dear wench, you have got my watch. Keep it for my sake as I shall never come back, and give my clothes to my poor old father.'

Richard Overfield stood trial for the murder of his son at the Lent Assizes in Shrewsbury on 19 March 1824, before Mr Justice Park. Mr Slaney led the prosecution, while Mr Corbett appeared for the defence.

The proceedings opened with Richard Overfield challenging three of the members of the jury, who were quickly replaced. He pleaded 'Not guilty' to the murder of baby Richard and it was immediately pointed out that, since Overfield was married, his wife would not be permitted to testify in court, either for or against him.

The prosecution then called Louisa Davies to the stand to describe the events of 21 September to the court and to relate how she found the phial of sulphuric acid hidden behind the garden fence.

Thomas Southwell was then called and recounted his conversation with the accused on the morning after the infant's death. Given that Overfield's son had died so tragically only the day before, he had been surprised to see Overfield in work that day. He then told the court about the use of vitriol in the carpet factory, stating that, as a labourer and not a dyer, Overfield had no legitimate business in the room where it was stored.

The liquid was normally kept in a small room adjoining the factory's dye-house and only the dyers were permitted access to it. However, the door to the storeroom was normally kept unlocked during the day and led directly onto the yard in which Overfield usually worked. The liquid was kept in a large, glass bottle that weighed several hundredweight when full. Southwell told the court that it was impossible for Overfield not to have heard of oil of vitriol as he had told the doctor and that it was equally impossible for him not to have known where it was kept in the factory. Southwell concluded by stating that Overfield was a quiet, hard-working and peaceable man. Clement Hughes, a second superintendent at the carpet factory, said exactly the same thing.

Mary Nichols testified to seeing Overfield walk down the garden and bend down on the day of his son's death. Mr Hall, Mr Spry and Mr Dugard were called as medical witnesses, while PC Edward Goodall gave details of Overfield's arrest.

Mr Justice Park then asked Overfield whether he had anything to say in his own defence. Initially, Overfield appeared not to understand what was being asked of him but he finally stated that all he wished to say was that he was innocent of the crime. Mr Corbett stated that he did not intend to call any witnesses for the defence, at which the judge summed up the case for the jury.

Such was the evidence against the accused that the jury took only two or three minutes of discussion to return a verdict of 'Guilty'. Mr Justice Park then put on his black cap and addressed the prisoner:

> Richard Overfield, you have been convicted after a most full and satisfactory trial on evidence that has left no doubt on the mind of any man who has heard it of the murder of your own child, the fruit of your body and whom you were bound by every tie of nature to protect and cherish.

The judge then advised the court of circumstances which, until then, he had been unable to reveal. Baby Richard had been conceived out of wedlock and, as a result, Overfield had been forced into marriage. Consequently, he had hated the child and had often told his wife that he 'would not support her or her bastard.'

Almost overcome with emotion, Mr Justice Park then told Overfield that he personally could not imagine how anyone could administer poison to an innocent child, knowing the agony it would cause. He fervently hoped that, in the six months that he had spent in prison while awaiting his trial, Overfield had had the opportunity to reflect on his actions and to pray for forgiveness.

Overfield himself stood rigid in the dock, expressing no emotion as he heard the judge sentence him to be hanged by the neck until dead. However, in the short time remaining to him before his eventual execution on 22 March 1824, he apparently became 'the very emblem of guilt and wretchedness'.

3

'MY LORD JUDGE, LET ME CALL MY WITNESSES'

Market Drayton, 1827

[The following rather complex case features no less than five defendants, most of whom were related either to their fellow defendants or to the principal witnesses. In order to better understand the case, the relationships between the defendants and witnesses are outlined below:

John Cox senior (defendant) was the father of **John Cox** junior and **Robert Cox** (defendants).
Ann Harris (defendant) was the mother of **Thomas Ellson** (witness). Thomas Ellson, nicknamed 'Shooler', was married to **Elizabeth** (witness), who was the daughter of John Cox senior and sister of John Cox junior and Robert Cox.]

In 1827, sheep rustling was rife in the area around Market Drayton, much of it the work of one gang. The gang had seven regular members, most of whom were related to one another. The oldest member was sixty-year-old John Cox, who also worked as a shoemaker. John was joined in his clandestine activities by his two sons, John junior and Robert, along with Joseph Pugh, Thomas Ellson, James Harrison and Ann Harris. The police were aware of the gang's misdemeanours but lacked sufficient evidence to bring a successful prosecution against them. Hence an appeal was made for information, which prompted twenty-one-year-old James Harrison to come forward with evidence against a fellow gang member, Thomas Ellson.

Newton, Market Drayton. (Author's collection)

As a result of information provided by Harrison, Ellson was arrested. However, when he came to stand trial, Harrison, who was due to appear as a principal witness for the prosecution, was nowhere to be found. It was assumed that he had either been bought off or had been too afraid to testify. Without Harrison's crucial testimony, the case against Ellson collapsed and he was acquitted.

Although Harrison seemed to have disappeared from the area without trace, his absence caused little concern as it was thought that he had simply decided to lie low for a while, avoiding any possible repercussions arising from informing on Thomas Ellson. It was not until Ellson was arrested on another unrelated matter that Harrison's true whereabouts came to light.

Faced with imprisonment, Ellson too turned informant, offering to tell magistrates what had happened to Harrison in exchange for his release. Ellson maintained that Harrison had been killed in order to silence him and implicated Joseph Pugh and Ann Harris in Harrison's murder. Pugh and Harris were both arrested and, as a result of information received from Thomas Ellson, police dug up a field in search of Harrison's body. Yet, although a patch of ground 10 yards by 12 yards was dug to a depth of 6ft, no remains were found.

Ann Harris was released from custody, but John Pugh was held for further questioning. Presumably keen to save his own skin, Pugh offered to show the police where the body of James Harrison was buried, and on 29 June 1827 he led police to a field on a farm owned by Mr Hocknell and directed them to a particular spot. Four feet below the surface, at the spot Pugh had indicated, was found the body of a man.

The body, which was fully clothed, was carefully excavated and taken to Market Drayton Poor House. There, James Harrison's father, John, viewed the decomposed remains and identified them as his son by a patch on the boots and by the hair. He was accompanied to the viewing by his wife, Sarah, James's stepmother, who also recognised her stepson's boots and a waistcoat, which she had washed and mended for James shortly before his disappearance.

Surgeon John Hopkins, from Market Drayton, had been called to the field immediately after the body had been uncovered and had supervised its removal to the Poor House. After Mr and Mrs Harrison had positively identified the remains, Hopkins conducted a post-mortem examination. He found the remains too decomposed to allow him to ascertain exactly how Harrison had met his death and whether or not violence had been used against him. However, the mere fact that the body had been buried suggested foul play rather than death by accident, suicide or natural causes, and, once their activities came under close scrutiny from the police, the gang members showed no loyalty towards each other. Each member willingly informed on the others and eventually Joseph Pugh, John Cox junior and Robert Cox were arrested and charged with murdering James Harrison on or about 17 July 1827. Ann Harris and John Cox senior were charged with being accessories to murder and also with inciting the other three accused to commit murder.

The defendants were brought for trial at the Shropshire Assizes in August 1828. The trial was presided over by Mr Justice Gaselee, with Mr Richards and Mr Whateley prosecuting. Mr J. Jervis appeared for John Cox senior and Robert Cox and Mr C. Phillips appeared for Ann Harris. Joseph Pugh and John Cox junior were undefended at the start of the proceedings and, on their behalf, Mr Phillips asked the judge if the court could appoint a counsel for them. Mr Justice Gaselee said that he could only do this if the defendants requested him to do so and, after both men had expressed a wish to be defended, Mr Gaselee instructed Mr Bather to act for them.

The defendants were apparently a fearsome group of people. John Cox senior was described in the *Shrewsbury Chronicle* as 'forbidding in countenance and demeanour', having a 'squalid face', which showed 'deep traces of revenge, malice and low cunning'. His sons, John and Robert, were merely described as 'ill-looking'. Joseph Pugh had 'a gypsy cast of features' and a 'look of savage fierceness', while Ann Harris had a 'most malignant pair of sparkling black eyes'.

Undeterred by their appearance, Mr Richards first outlined what few facts were known about the case and, having called Harrison's father and stepmother and surgeon John Hopkins to testify about the remains found buried in the field, Richards then called on a number of witnesses to describe what he believed were Harrison's last moments alive.

Harrison had lodged with George Pugh – the father of defendant Joseph – at Little Drayton Common. George's wife, Ann, told the court that the last time she had seen James Harrison he had been wearing a blue coat and trousers with a striped waistcoat. She had viewed the body found in the field and believed that it was that of James Harrison, basing her identification on the clothes that the deceased was wearing.

George Pugh stated that, to the best of his knowledge, the last time he had seen Harrison alive was on the evening of 14 July 1827. Harrison had been sitting in front of the fire with Joseph Pugh and at eleven o'clock that night George and Ann had retired to bed, leaving the two men downstairs. (Although both Harrison and Joseph lodged at George Pugh's home, there were no beds for them and they slept either on chairs or on the floor.) Both Ann and George Pugh testified to hearing John Cox senior making threats against James Harrison approximately three weeks before his disappearance.

At one o'clock on the morning of 15 July, George Pugh was awakened by a loud whistle coming from outside his house. Gallantly, he had awakened his wife and demanded that she went to the window to see what was happening. Ann did as she was told. The whistle was repeated two or three times and, as Ann looked out of the window, she saw young John Cox, who was 'skulched' under the hedge as if to try and remain out of sight. Shortly afterwards, George and Ann heard footsteps downstairs in their cottage, although the noise of movement soon stopped, allowing them to resume their interrupted sleep.

When Ann went downstairs the following morning, she found Joseph Pugh asleep in a chair. She wakened him and asked him where James Harrison was, to which Joseph replied that he had left.

Thomas Ellson was called to the witness box and stated that he had come from Shrewsbury Gaol. The previous year he had been an inmate at Stafford Gaol where he was serving a sentence for stealing potatoes. On his release from Stafford, he had gone straight to Shrewsbury Gaol, where he was held for three months on a charge of sheep stealing. He was released after being acquitted at the assizes, after which he married Elizabeth Cox.

On his release from prison, Robert Cox had told him that, if it weren't for him and Joseph Pugh, Ellson would have been hung. Robert had demanded money from Ellson's mother, Ann Harris, by way of a thank you and was eventually reluctantly given 2s and told in no uncertain terms never to bother Ann Harris again.

Ellson, who was nicknamed 'Shooler', then told the court of a conversation between himself, Joseph Pugh and John Cox junior. According to Ellson, Pugh had told him that he had lured James Harrison out of his father's house on the pretext of going to steal some bacon. When they reached a prearranged point, Pugh told Harrison that they were too early to steal the bacon and must wait a while. He persuaded Harrison to lie down by a haystack, where the Cox boys were already waiting. They had jumped Harrison, slipped a twisted string around his neck and pulled on it until he was dead. Harrison's last words had been, 'Oh, Lord, spare my life and I'll not hurt Shooler'. Once he was dead, he was dragged into the field and buried.

Ellson maintained that John Cox senior had approached him while Ellson was in the lock-up at Market Drayton on a charge of stealing fowl. Cox had promised him that, if he said nothing of what he knew about the murder then Cox would

Stafford Gaol, c. 1900. (Author's collection)

pay for him to be defended on his current charge. Ellson also stated that his mother, Ann Harris, and John Cox senior had each paid the Cox boys 50s to have Harrison murdered.

Cross-examined, Ellson admitted that he realised that the charge against his mother, Ann Harris, was a capital offence and that she would hang if found guilty. Professing not to know whether he would benefit from his mother's will should she be hanged, he assured the court that he was there today for the sake of public justice, not to save himself from being transported or from having to face any charges relating to other offences.

Next to take the witness stand was Charles Warren, an attorney from Market Drayton. He had taken Joseph Pugh's evidence, which he said Pugh had given on the understanding that he would not be hanged for the murder of James Harrison. The defence lawyers promptly objected to the inclusion of this evidence, since Pugh had evidently been offered an inducement to make his statement. The prosecution did not argue the objection and next called Thomas Twemloe, a Shropshire magistrate, who had taken a statement from both Joseph Pugh and Ann Harris.

Again, the counsel for the defence objected, on the grounds that, as a magistrate, Twemloe would know Mr Warren and it could therefore be assumed that the inducement offered by Warren in obtaining Pugh's first confession had not been retracted. Mr Justice Gaselee upheld the objection as far as it applied to Joseph Pugh, but stated that Ann Harris's alleged confession to Mr Twemloe could be heard.

The prosecution then called or recalled several witnesses who had heard Joseph Pugh confess to killing Harrison without first having been offered any incentive to do so. These witnesses included PC Henry Holt, who stated that Pugh had told him that he and John Cox junior had murdered Harrison, while Robert Cox looked on. Pugh and John Cox had then buried the body.

Revd David Edwards had seen Joseph Pugh in custody and testified that Pugh had told him exactly the same thing. Pugh had apparently also confessed to Mr Warren at the inquest.

Joseph Taylor, who had arrested John Cox junior for his part in the murder, had heard a slightly different account. John had told him that he and Joseph Pugh had carried out the killing together and that his brother, Robert, had not even been present when Harrison was murdered. PC Edward Simminster corroborated Taylor's evidence.

The confession made by Ann Harris was then read out to the court. Harris said that, when her son had been arrested for sheep stealing, she had approached John Cox senior and told him that they should 'do something' about James Harrison. (It must be remembered that, in those days, sheep stealing was still a capital offence and, if convicted, Thomas Ellson might have hanged for his crime – at very least, he would have been transported.) Harris and Cox had discussed various ways of preventing Harrison from testifying against Ellson, including poisoning him, pushing him into a coal pit and cutting his throat. Ann Harris had later tried unsuccessfully to persuade her sister-in-law to buy sixpennyworth of poison for her, saying that she intended to use it on Harrison. Eventually Robert Cox, who was present at the time, had asked Ann if she would give him 2s to 'get Harrison out of the way'. Ann agreed to this and was later to meet Robert at his father's home, giving him three half crowns and some meat in payment for the cold-blooded assassination of the principal witness against her son. Knowing that Harrison was about to be killed, Ann Harris left her shovel standing outside her cottage for several days and nights so that the murderers could use it to bury the body. She got up one morning to find the shovel covered in dirt and bearing traces of blood and hair.

Elizabeth Ellson testified to walking with her mother-in-law and Joseph Pugh to visit her husband, Thomas, in Stafford Gaol. On the walk, the conversation between Harris and Pugh had revolved around ways off getting rid of James Harrison. Harris had offered Pugh 6s and a coat if he would kill Harrison. On arrival at the prison, Elizabeth recalled that Ann had reassured her son, telling him to be content, as 'they' couldn't hurt him. Ann made a point of asking a warder if Thomas would be acquitted if Harrison didn't testify against him. The warder, Thomas Followes, testified that he could recollect the conversation but that he could not recall everything that was said.

On the day of the discovery of the body, Robert Cox had been arrested while hiding in a field of growing corn, trying desperately to evade capture. Robert had named Joseph Pugh as the man who had killed James Harrison.

The case for the prosecution complete, the defendants were called upon to address the court. Joseph Pugh insisted that Ann Harris had poisoned James Harrison and that she had given Pugh and John Cox junior 50s to bury him. John Cox junior made a similar statement while his brother, Robert, swore that he was as innocent as an unborn child.

Mr Jervis, counsel for John Cox senior, told the judge that he believed that there was insufficient evidence against his client to ask him to offer any defence. However, Mr Justice Gaselee disagreed and Cox merely stated dispiritedly that he did not wish to call any witnesses.

Finally Ann Harris was given her chance to speak. Ann seemed resigned to her fate but told the court she would have liked to call one witness, Ann Mountford. This witness was not called, but Ann's defence attorney did call two witnesses to testify on her behalf. The first of these was an attorney, Mr Stanley, who produced a copy of a will made by Harris's mother, Mrs Mary Roden. Under the terms of the will, Ann Harris was left property of considerable worth, which was to be divided amongst her children in the event of her death. The defence counsel also called another attorney, Richard Asterley. Asterley had seen Thomas Ellson in Stafford Gaol and told the court that Ellson had said that he intended to give evidence in this case in order to save himself from transportation. Thus, both of Ann's witnesses offered a valid reason for Thomas Ellson to testify against his mother.

Mr Justice Gaselee summarised the evidence for the jurors who retired for a short while before returning with verdicts of 'Guilty' against John Cox junior, Robert Cox and Joseph Pugh. The foreman of the jury informed the court that they had not yet been able to reach a decision on Ann Harris and John Cox senior. The judge asked them to deliberate further and, after a few more minutes, the jury returned with verdicts of 'Guilty of being accessories to murder' against both defendants.

At this, Mr Justice Gaselee asked them if they would reconsider their verdict on John Cox senior. The judge re-read all the evidence pertaining to Cox to the jury and had just finished doing so when Cox himself piped up from the dock.

'My Lord Judge, my Lord Judge, I'll speak, I'll speak now. That lawyer chap and that there counsellor, they a'kept my witnesses out of court and would not call them. They would not and I have them to call.' [*sic*]

Mr Jervis told the judge that he had simply exercised his discretion and if he had done wrong, then it was his responsibility.

'My Lord Judge, let me call my witnesses,' begged Cox and the judge capitulated.

The first witness to be called for John Cox was Mr Reeves, a sawyer. Reeves stated that all he knew about the business was that something had passed between Pugh and Cox and that there had been an agreement that Cox would become answerable to the charge of murder with Pugh for a pair of shoes. The court was left bemused by Mr Reeves's testimony, failing to see how what he had said could possibly have been so important to the defence that Mr Cox had deemed it vital to call Reeves as a witness.

Next, Mr Cox asked that George Pugh should be recalled as a witness for him. Pugh was eventually located but his testimony added little to Cox's defence since he simply stated that he knew nothing about the job. Cox then asked him about a conversation Pugh had supposedly had with Thomas Ellson, to which Pugh replied that he had never spoken with Ellson.

At this, an exasperated John Cox gave up, telling the court that it was no use asking questions if people wouldn't tell the truth.

The jury retired for the third time, returning to say that their verdict on John Cox senior was unchanged. As far as they were concerned, he was guilty.

The judge then sentenced all of the defendants to be hanged, their bodies to be dissected afterwards.

In the event, both John Cox senior and his son, Robert, were reprieved at the last moment. Twenty-six-year-old John Cox junior and nineteen-year-old Joseph Pugh were hanged at Shrewsbury on 4 August 1828.

Ann Harris's execution was slightly delayed while her lawyers appealed her conviction. However, on 16 August 1828, aged fifty, she became the first woman to be hanged at Shrewsbury Prison in twenty-five years.

4

'MY LIFE IS GONE'

Beckbury, 1833

On 18 July 1833, the haymaking was in full swing at the farms around the village of Beckbury and everyone who was available had been roped in to assist. One such person was George Hayward, the son of the local butcher, who had spent a long, hot day helping to build hayricks. At frequent intervals during the day, he had refreshed himself with draughts of beer and, by the end of the day, had imbibed rather more alcohol than was strictly necessary merely to quench his thirst.

That evening, George decided to pay court to one of the young women of the village and appeared unannounced and uninvited at the house where she lived with her widowed mother. Mrs Causer was not at all in favour of the prospect of a courtship between Hayward and her daughter, but he seemed insensitive to her disapproval and, having been allowed into the house, had long outstayed any small welcome he might have received. Mrs Causer tried her best to persuade him to leave but eventually she was forced to send for her son, John, to forcibly eject him.

John did exactly that. Without saying a word, he took hold of Hayward by his shoulders, spun him round to face the door and propelled him to the threshold, where he delivered a hearty kick to Hayward's backside.

Hayward lodged with Maria Meeson, who lived only 300-400 yards from the Causer's home. At some time between nine and ten o'clock that evening, Maria heard George Hayward entering the house through the window of his bedroom, his normal way of entering and exiting. Hayward crossed the kitchen into the pantry, where Maria heard him briefly rummaging about as if looking for something. He then went back to his bedroom and left the house, again climbing through the window.

Moments later, Maria heard raised voices in the street outside her home. A voice she recognised as John Causer's said, 'You shall not go down there any more tonight, making a disturbance', to which George Hayward promptly replied that he had property there and intended to fetch it.

Beckbury. (© N. Sly, 2008)

Causer asked what property Hayward had in the village, saying that he would escort Hayward and, if no property was found, bring him straight back again to his lodgings.

Hayward shouted, 'Blast your eyes!' and Maria, along with passers-by on the street, heard the sound of a blow being struck. The next thing they heard was Causer shouting, 'Murder! Murder!' at the top of his voice.

Moments later, John Causer burst through his mother's front door, telling the startled woman, 'My life is gone.' The front of his shirt was soaked with blood and when his mother prised his hands away from his belly, she noticed a large stab wound, through which his intestines were protruding. Meanwhile, George Hayward had walked calmly back to his lodgings, undressed and retired to his bed.

A doctor was immediately summoned and Mr T.E. Fletcher, a surgeon from Shifnal, arrived in Beckbury sometime between eleven o'clock and midnight. He found John Causer lying on his bed, faint through loss of blood, with one stab wound in his belly and another on his shoulder. Causer asked the surgeon if he was in danger and the surgeon had to admit that he was. By the following morning, Causer had become feverish and restless and the surgeon called in the local rector, Revd W. Bates.

Both men were aware that Causer would not survive and decided that they should take a deposition from the dying man. Having made sure that John Causer was well aware of the gravity of his condition, Revd Bates wrote down Causer's recollections of the previous evening:

> About the hour of nine on Thursday the 18th instant, deponent was sent for by his mother to turn George Hayward out of her house. A struggle ensued and deponent was successful in turning him out. Hayward on leaving the house said he would make the deponent remember it. Within five minutes after, deponent followed Hayward and took him his hat and met him opposite Mr Percival's barn 10 yards from his lodgings. Deponent said 'Here's your hat'. Hayward took his hat and said he should have his rights and stabbed him, saying it served him right and then ran away. Deponent says he saw something in his hand which appeared like a cutlass half a yard long. Dated 19 July 1833 and signed by the mark of John Causer. [*sic*]

Causer died soon after signing the deposition with his cross.

Hayward was immediately arrested and charged with the wilful murder of John Causer. He was committed for trial before Chief Justice Tidnal at the Shropshire Assizes, with Mr Corbett prosecuting the case and Mr Bather defending.

At the opening of the proceedings, George Hayward pleaded 'Not Guilty'. His defence counsel, Mr Bather, immediately approached the bench and called the judge's attention to rather sensational broadsheets that had been published after the

Beckbury Church. (© N. Sly, 2008)

murder by a Mr Walter of Ironbridge, who was actually one of the police constables involved in Causer's arrest. Bather was afraid that the 'false and exaggerated' content of the broadsheets was prejudicial to the case for the defence and asked the judge to poll the jury to ask if any of them had seen the publications.

Describing the publications as 'most indecent, particularly in an officer of justice', the judge vowed to ensure that the publisher would be 'removed from a situation he so unworthily fills.' He then told the jury that they should put aside anything they might have read or heard about the case and be guided only by what they heard in court in reaching their verdict. Since one of the jurors admitted to having heard a broadsheet read aloud, he was promptly dismissed and a replacement juror sworn in.

Once it finally began, the trial of George Hayward did not take long to reach a conclusion. The prosecution first called Mrs Causer, the victim's mother, and then Maria Meeson, the defendant's landlady, who both recalled the circumstances surrounding the death of John Causer. William Sutton, the schoolmaster at Beckbury, followed them into the witness box. He had been walking through the village on the night of the murder and had witnessed the confrontation between Causer and Hayward. His companion on that evening, Benjamin Adams, corroborated his testimony.

Surgeon Mr Fletcher told the court of his treatment of the victim and his findings at the post-mortem examination, which he had conducted. He had noted two stab wounds, most probably made by something resembling a large butcher's knife. Causer's intestines had protruded through the wound in his belly and Fletcher had recorded that they were perforated in two places.

Mr Bather then questioned the judge about Causer's deposition and its admissibility as evidence. He wanted reassurance that Causer had been fully aware of the fact that he was dying when the deposition was taken. Revd Bates and also Mr Fletcher, who had been present when the deposition was dictated to Bates, both assured the judge that Causer had been informed of the hopelessness of his condition beforehand. Although Causer had been in great pain and 'excited', Bates had made sure that he understood the importance of telling the truth and of giving as detailed an account as he possibly could. The deposition, said Bates, had been entirely Causer's own account and had not been in response to any questions put to him. Having made his deposition, it was read back to him and he had made some corrections.

Satisfied that the proper procedure had been followed, the judge allowed the deposition to be read to the court. (The 'cutlass' mentioned by the victim as the murder weapon had actually been one of four butcher's knives kept by Causer in the pantry at his lodgings.)

The final witness was a policeman who produced the defendant's clothes. However, he was not questioned.

The judge then addressed George Hayward, asking him if, having heard the evidence against him, he had anything to say to the jury in his own defence, to which Hayward simply answered 'No.'

The judge then instructed the jury, telling them that they should consider whether or not the stabbing of John Causer took place immediately after provocation. The kick delivered by John Causer in ejecting the defendant from his mother's home must be counted as provocation and, if the stabbing followed immediately afterwards, then the law, allowing for human weaknesses, would mitigate the offence from murder to manslaughter. However, in this case, it seemed that Hayward had walked back to his home and deliberately sought out a weapon with which to inflict injury on the deceased. Thus, the stabbing had hardly taken place in a 'paroxysm of passion'. Yet, asked the judge, had any further provocation occurred after both parties had left Mrs Causer's house? If the jury believed that it had, then they were entirely justified in returning a verdict of manslaughter against the accused, but, if they believed that the stabbing had not been committed 'in a gust of passion' but instead as an act of revenge for the previous insult, then it was their duty to return a verdict of wilful murder.

The jury consulted briefly before choosing the latter option and pronouncing George Hayward 'Guilty of wilful murder', after which the judge sentenced him to death by hanging, prescribing that his body should afterwards be buried within the confines of the prison walls. Hayward accepted the verdict and sentence without emotion, his eyes firmly fixed on the floor as they had been throughout the proceedings.

He was hanged, aged twenty, at Shrewsbury on 5 August 1833.

5

'LORD, RECEIVE MY SOUL'

Bronygarth, 1841

Sixty-seven-year-old spinster Emma Evans lived alone in Bronygarth, over the small general store that she ran. She was known to be extremely conscious about security. The shop door was always kept bolted and any customers had to knock for admittance. Once they were inside the shop, Emma would bolt the door behind them and only unlock it again when they were ready to leave. The takings from her shop were always kept in a little leather bag, which she hid between her feather bed and her mattress.

On 16 December 1841, Miss Evans served two customers at around five o'clock in the afternoon. The first was Thomas Eales, a young servant at the Britannia Inn, which was situated less than 100 yards from the little shop. Eales, who was a regular customer, bought ½oz of tea, for which he paid 2*d*. He had asked the time before he left there and been told that it was five o'clock. The second customer was nine-year-old Sarah Pearce, who had been sent on an errand to buy tea and sugar. Sarah clearly remembered hearing Emma Evans bolt the door behind her when she left.

Around half an hour later, a neighbour passed by the house and noticed a light in an upstairs room. It struck her as slightly unusual, since she was aware that the light was shining from the 'best' room, which was rarely, if ever, used.

At seven o'clock, Richard Hughes went to the shop. He knocked twice on the door but received no reply, so he went to the kitchen door and found it ajar. He knocked again and called out for Emma but there was no response.

The house was in total darkness and Hughes had no lamp. As he stood there wondering what he should do next, he saw a light coming up the street. It was a lantern, carried by Mrs Sarah Foulkes. Hughes drew her attention to the open door and they decided to go into the house to check up on Emma. As they walked into the kitchen, the first thing they saw was Miss Evans sprawled on the floor in a large pool of blood.

Richard Hughes took her arm and immediately realised that she was dead. He quickly ushered Mrs Foulkes outside and raised the alarm. Soon the house was full of concerned neighbours.

Mr Perkin, a surgeon from Chirk, arrived to examine the body at about twenty past eight that evening. He found that Emma's throat had been cut and that she had died as a result of blood loss. When he later conducted a detailed post-mortem examination, he also found three wounds on Emma's head and a wound on her lip. He surmised that Emma had been sitting in her chair by the fire, smoking her pipe, when she had been hit on the head from behind with a heavy instrument, which caused her to fall forward onto the floor, driving her tobacco pipe through her top lip. Perkin also found clear marks in blood on Emma's body made by the ridges of corduroy trousers.

He believed that Emma had been surprised by whoever had attacked her, as she did not appear to have fought for her life. Although her house had obviously been searched and left with linen and papers strewn about, the murderer had not found her leather purse, which was still in its usual position beneath the mattress. Miss Evans's pockets had been turned out and the contents of the shop till taken.

Meanwhile, at about nine o'clock, 4 or 5 miles away at Cefn Mawr, John Williams and Joseph Slawson walked into the King's Head public house. They asked for a pint of beer then told the landlady to make it a quart, as they were thirsty. The two men stayed at the pub drinking for about an hour then asked landlady, Sarah Bradeley, for some bread and cheese. She had none to offer them, so one of the men pulled some loose bacon out of his pocket and asked her to fry it for them, which she did.

As she left the kitchen to serve the men their bacon, she noticed a large bundle on a bench. She tried to check its contents, but was unable to untie it, so asked to whom it belonged. The two men said that it was theirs and Sarah asked them to move it, saying that she could not be held responsible if it was stolen. 'Jack, go and fetch it,' said Slawson and the bundle was moved into the parlour.

Williams and Slawson left the pub at ten o'clock. Their appearance had aroused the suspicions of the landlord and landlady, as both men were liberally splashed with mud, so William Bradeley, the landlord's son, and his brother-in-law, Thomas Davies, decided to follow them. They caught up with the two men after following them for about three quarters of a mile and Thomas Davies tried to apprehend them, at which Williams and Slawson dropped the bundle and fled. Bradeley took the bundle back to the King's Head and called the local police constable. When opened, the bundle was found to contain several pieces of property later identified as belonging to Emma Evans.

Williams and Slawson seemed to have vanished into thin air and *The Times* newspaper of 24 December 1841 theorised that they were 'concealed in some of the wretched dwellings with which Wrexham abounds, which are inhabited by a numerous and desperate set of thieves and bad characters.' Police in all the neighbouring counties were alerted and a reward was offered for the capture of the two fugitives, yet it was not in Wrexham that the two men were apprehended but in Coventry.

On 23 December, John Williams walked into the premises of silversmith Mr Fridlander in Fleet Street, Coventry and asked him if he bought old silver. When Fridlander said that he did, Williams took a broken teaspoon out of his pocket. The silversmith told Williams that he didn't buy plate from anyone unless he knew them, to which Williams replied that his name was Edward Jones and that he lived locally at Spon Street.

Williams was paid 2s for the spoon and returned to the shop on the following day, this time trying to sell ten similar teaspoons and a pair of sugar tongs. All the items were monogrammed with the initials 'E.E.' and, having confirmed his customer's name as Edward Jones, the silversmith pointed out that the spoons and tongs obviously didn't belong to him. 'Mr Jones' told him that the spoons were a gift from a relation, Edward Edwards.

Mr Fridlander weighed the items and made an offer of £1 5s for them. He then pretended that he had no change in the shop and asked Jones to call back in half an hour for his money. In the meantime, he went straight to the Chief Constable of Coventry, Mr Prosser.

Unfortunately, Mr Prosser was out and Fridlander had to stall his customer for a further twenty-four hours. On 25 December – Christmas Day – Prosser waited in a back room at Mr Fridlander's premises, observing the shop through a small window. When Mr Jones came to collect his money, Prosser stepped into the shop and greeted him with the words, 'Hello, Williams'.

Having securely handcuffed his quarry, Mr Prosser proceeded to search Williams there and then, finding a German silver caddy spoon and two knives in his pockets. There was also a piece of paper on which was written the words, 'You must make the best of your way through South Wales to the Bristol Channel and cross over to Cornwall and enquire at Tregonna for some of the Beards, if you are lucky enough to get there.'

Prosser went to the house at Spon End, where Williams had been lodging, and retrieved his clothes, which included a torn shirt that was stained with blood. At the lodging house, he found the wife of Joseph Slawson, who surrendered a small gilt ring, telling the officer that it had been a gift from her husband.

Prosser tracked Slawson down to the Crown and Kettle pub in Fleet Street. He approached him with the words 'Well, Slawson, how are you?'

'Middling', replied Slawson.

Slawson's clothes were also seized, including a pair of corduroy trousers that had been left with a local tailor and were bloodstained.

Arrangements were made to transport Williams and Slawson by train and coach back to Shrewsbury, where they were detained in the gaol at the Guildhall before being brought before magistrates and committed for trial at the next Shrewsbury Assizes. While in custody awaiting his trial, Williams tried to escape from his prison

A postcard of Shrewsbury. (Author's collection)

cell, taking a staple from his hammock and using it to remove bricks from the cell wall.

The trial opened before Mr Justice Patterson on 21 March. Mr F.V. Lee and Mr W.H. Cooke prosecuted the case and while Mr Yardley acted as counsel for the defence on behalf of Joseph Slawson, Williams was undefended.

Having initially maintained that they had found the bundle of Miss Evans's possessions on the roadside, both Williams and Slawson eventually confessed to committing the robbery, each denying any involvement in the murder and blaming the other for killing Miss Evans.

Slawson's defence counsel assured the court that his client had agreed only to carry out the robbery and had never even considered the possibility of a murder being committed, even though it was believed that he had struck the first blow to the victim's head as she sat by the fire enjoying a quiet smoke. Somewhat unfairly, the eventual verdict of the jury was that John Williams was 'Guilty of the wilful murder of Emma Evans', for which he received the death penalty. Slawson was convicted only of stealing goods and chattels and was sentenced to seven years transportation.

Hence only twenty-four-year-old John Williams kept an appointment with executioner Mr Taylor at the Salop County Gaol on 2 April 1842. As he stood on the gallows awaiting his death, he apparently repeated the words, 'Lord, receive my soul' over and over again until the bolt was finally drawn.

His death was instantaneous and, after his body had hung for the customary one hour, it was examined by two artists from the local Coalport China factory, who had been granted permission by the sheriff to take casts of his face.

6

'OH DEAR, HOW ILL I AM'

Whixall, 1841

Arthur Williams and his wife, Mary, lived in a cottage in Whixall, near Wem. They shared their home with their daughter, Eliza and her husband, a brick maker named Thomas Harries. Thomas had previously been widowed and consequently, on her marriage, Eliza had become stepmother to the two children borne by his first wife. Arthur and Mary accepted the children into their home, but had been unable to resist interfering in their upbringing. This infuriated their son-in-law, who vowed that he would 'remember them for it.'

On 18 December 1841, Mary Williams cooked a pig's fry for supper. The two families used the same kitchen, although they ate in separate rooms and flour was usually transferred into two bags, one each for the use of the two women in the household. Mary took some flour from her striped bag in the kitchen and used it to thicken her gravy. Within five minutes of eating his meal, Arthur began to feel very unwell. His stomach swelled and he eventually felt so ill that he retired to bed, where he spent an uncomfortable night vomiting.

When he awoke the next morning, he still felt far from well and had no appetite for food. Hence he didn't eat any of the apple dumpling that his wife cooked for dinner. Within minutes of eating her portion of the dumpling, Mary rose from the table, complaining, 'Oh dear, how ill I am.' Soon she was retching violently, vomiting up 'green and yellow stuff' and frothing at the mouth. Her daughter went with her to the outside privy since Mary was unable to walk there and back without assistance. She continued to vomit for the rest of the afternoon and was put to bed at about five o'clock. Still feeling ill himself, Arthur also went to bed at the same time but got up just before nine o'clock as his wife's condition was obviously worsening. She died minutes later and, after her death, Arthur heard Thomas Harries say to

Eliza, 'There's something in that flour.' Strangely, at no time during her, admittedly brief, illness and death was a doctor called to treat Mary Williams.

Mr Thomas Norway Arthur and Dr Thomas Groom carried out a post-mortem examination on the body of Mary Williams. Before her death, Mary had been a healthy woman, with the exception of a 'little fullness of the vessels of the left lung'. Now, her stomach was found to contain a large quantity of greenish-yellow matter and the stomach lining had taken on a milky appearance, similar to the white of an egg. There were large patches of inflammation on the walls of the stomach and the doctors concluded that she had consumed some sort of corrosive poison, which, from their observations, they believed to be arsenic. Mr Arthur notified the police of his suspicions and Constable Richard Jones went to the Williams's house. Finding Thomas Harries at work, he arrested Eliza and took her into custody at his own house. When he finished work, Thomas Harries came looking for his wife.

Jones asked Harries where he normally kept the arsenic and was told that it was kept in the buttery. In the company of PC Edward Hughes, Jones escorted Harries back to the Williams' house where Harries produced an empty bottle, telling the police that he had used the entire contents for poisoning mice. The police took samples from the bags of flour and also removed a saltbox from the house. Jones then arrested Thomas Harries, telling him, 'The Lord have mercy on you Thomas, for it is a dreadful deed you have done.' At this, Thomas began to cry and agreed, 'It is.'

The stomach and its contents were boxed and sent to analyst Mr Thomas Blunt, along with the flour taken by the police from the bags in the kitchen. Blunt found large quantities of arsenic to be present in Mary's bag of flour and also in the stomach contents, although not in such large amounts. The amount of arsenic in Mary's stomach was, however, more than sufficient to constitute a fatal dose. Having received the results of Blunt's analyses, the two doctors determined that Mary Williams' death had been caused by ingestion of arsenic.

Eliza Harries had also made an apple dumpling on the same day as her mother and the two dumplings had been wrapped in the same cloth, with a piece of string separating them and then boiled in the same pot. Eliza, Thomas and the two children had consumed her dumpling without any ill effects, a fact that they pointed out at the inquest into Mary Williams's death, held before coroner Mr Joseph Dickens. However, two witnesses were produced at the inquest who had seen Eliza make her dumpling and both testified that she had taken the flour that she used from a different bag. It was also pointed out at the inquest that, on the morning after Mary's death, someone had suggested feeding the leftover half of her dumpling that Arthur had felt too ill to eat, to the Harries children. Eliza had twice refused to allow this, although she later said that she had given the children the remains of her mother's dumpling and that they had eaten it. Since Thomas Harries had purchased arsenic recently for the purpose of killing mice, he was charged with the wilful murder of Mary Williams and Eliza was charged with assisting him. Magistrates subsequently committed both for trial at the next assizes, but Eliza, who was at that time heavily pregnant, died in prison before she could be brought to trial.

The remains of Mary William's dumpling had not been fed to the Harries children as their stepmother had said but had in fact been given to a neighbour, Elizabeth Minshall. Mrs Minshall gave the dumpling to her son, John Haycock, who went to his canal boat after eating it. He too began to vomit and was very ill – in fact *The Times* was to report that he had died and had become 'the second victim of this unparalleled atrocity'. However, since he was later to give evidence at the trial of Thomas Harries, it appears that reports of his demise were somewhat exaggerated.

The trial opened on 22 March 1842 before Mr Justice Patterson, with Mr F.V. Lee and Mr W.H. Cooke prosecuting. Thomas Harries, who pleaded 'Not Guilty', was not defended.

Arthur Williams was the first witness called. He described his own illness, followed by his wife's illness and subsequent death. He also testified to the fact that Thomas Harries kept arsenic in the house and that he had seen him mixing it with grease to use for poisoning mice. Williams told the court that sugar of lead was also kept at his home and was used for treating cows. He then said that Thomas Harries had recently made a trip to Ellesmere and that he had asked Harries to buy some 'Barbados turpentine' for him while he was there.

Next to testify was John Edwards, who had visited the house on the morning that both women made their apple dumplings and noticed that the flour for the two dumplings had been taken from different bags. The prosecution then called Mary Jones, whose cottage adjoined that of Arthur Williams.

She testified that Mary Williams and Thomas Harries frequently fought about the children and related that Harries had often threatened to 'knock the old woman's brains out' if she persisted in interfering. On one occasion, Mary Williams had made a trip to Whitchurch in heavy snow and there had been concerns about her safety. According to Mary Jones, Harries had said that he wished she might be found stiff on the side of the road.

Elizabeth Minshall and her son, John Haycock, told the court of receiving the remains of Mary Williams's dumpling and of John becoming extremely ill after eating it. Then Joseph Williams, Arthur's brother, stated that he had heard Harries saying that Mrs Williams ought to be poisoned.

Next to testify was Joseph Vaughan, an assistant to Mr Lee, a druggist from Ellesmere. He recalled a man coming into his employer's shop about a month before the death of Mary Williams and asking for 'Barbados turpentine'. Vaughan had told his customer that there was no such thing. He had then sold 2oz of arsenic to the same man for the purpose of poisoning mice. Vaughan had been taken to see Thomas Harries in prison but had been unable to identify him as the customer who had bought arsenic.

Richard Jones told the court of the arrest of Thomas and Eliza Harries and he was followed into the witness box by his colleague, Edward Hughes, whose evidence caused quite a stir in court.

Hughes said that, at the inquest into Mary's death, Thomas Harries had needed to leave the room and he had accompanied him into the garden where Harries had commented that it was a hard thing to suffer for what another person had done. When Hughes asked him what he meant, Harries told him that it was his wife, Eliza, who had poisoned her mother and that she had confessed it to him after the old lady's death. Harries said that he had told his wife not to say anything to the police and that Eliza had since sworn her innocence and accused him of poisoning her mother.

The medical witnesses then testified, with Mr Blunt going into great detail about the methods he had used to establish the presence of arsenic in Mary Williams's remains and in the flour taken from her house. The prosecution then rested and Thomas Harries was asked if he would like to address the jury in his own defence.

Harries said that he had hoped, begged and prayed that the truth might be heard in court, but that he had not heard it spoken that day. He then sensationally accused Arthur Williams of taking his wife's life on account of her bad temper and jealousy and also said that he had heard Arthur offering his daughter, Eliza, 1s if she would poison her mother. Laying the blame for the old lady's death firmly on his deceased wife and his father-in-law, Harries maintained that his son, John, who had been sent to the workhouse after the arrest of his father and stepmother, could corroborate his story. Harries then asked the jury to consider the fact that he had eaten the dumpling made by his wife, which had been boiled in the same pan as the poisoned dumpling. Would he have done so, he asked, if he had known that there was anything even slightly suspicious about the dumpling made by his mother-in-law?

At this, the judge asked why young John Harries was not in court. The boy's uncle, Samuel Egerton, who was married to Thomas Harries's sister, told him that he had been supposed to bring the child to court but that the relieving officer at the Wem workhouse would not allow him to do so.

The judge then issued a subpoena for John Harries and sent a court officer to Wem with it, instructing him to return with the boy. The court was adjourned for three hours until the child arrived.

Nine-year-old John was questioned by the judge to ensure that he knew the difference between telling the truth and telling a lie and that he understood the consequences of not telling the truth. When it was apparent that he did, he was allowed to testify. The boy told the court that his 'mother' (Eliza) and his 'grandmother' frequently had 'bad words' and were not friends. He had also heard cross words spoken between his 'grandfather' and 'grandmother' saying that on one occasion Arthur had threatened to kick his wife. Speaking of the day on which Mary was taken ill and died, John told the court that Arthur had said that it was useless sending for a doctor to attend to her, as she would be dead in a few hours time.

After hearing John's testimony, the judge asked for several witnesses to be recalled. The first of these was Arthur Williams, who categorically denied having words with his wife, saying that they lived as comfortably together as a man and wife could do. He stated that he had not said anything about it being useless to call a doctor to attend to his wife and he also denied any animosity between his wife and daughter. Finally, he assured the court that he had no idea where his son-in-law kept the arsenic other than that he had seen him bringing it out of the pantry.

Analyst Mr Blunt was then recalled and stated that he had found no sugar of lead present in the remains of Mary William, this being the poison that Arthur Williams admitted to having in the house for the purpose of treating cows. Blunt then said that, had Mary Williams's dumpling been poisoned, he would have expected that poison to leach out into the water in which the dumpling was boiled. However, arsenic was a poison that was 'at all times difficult of solution' and was repelled by unctuous substances, therefore it should not have unduly affected the other dumpling, cooked at the same time in the same pot.

Finally, Mary Jones was recalled to the stand and, asked specifically about the relationship between Eliza Harries and Mary Williams. She admitted that there were frequent quarrels between the two women.

The judge then summarised the case for the jury, commenting that the evidence given by young John Harries might well have thrown a different light on the case in the minds of the jurors. He pointed out that, although Thomas Harries had, in the past, implied that his wife had poisoned her mother, today was the first time he had implicated his father-in-law in the death of the old lady. Mr Justice Patterson then went through all the evidence and instructed the jury that if they had any doubt at all then they must give the prisoner the benefit of it.

The jury remained in court during their deliberations, at one stage turning to look at Thomas Harries who immediately told them, 'I hope you will have mercy on me, gentlemen'. In the event, this was exactly what happened as, within five minutes, the foreman of the jury announced a verdict of 'Not Guilty'.

Harries was discharged from the court and nobody else was ever charged with causing the death of the old lady by the administration of arsenic. Thus the poisoning of Mary Williams remains an unsolved mystery to this day.

[Note: In various contemporary accounts of this case, the names of the mother and daughter are transposed. Thus the victim is alternatively called Mary or Eliza Williams while her daughter is named Eliza or Mary Harries. The surname Harries is also spelled Harris in several of the newspaper accounts.]

7

'FOUND DEAD'

Pontesbury, 1845

Elisabeth Preece could hardly be described as a paragon of virtue, since she had two illegitimate children and, by July 1845, was pregnant with her third. Yet Elisabeth had no need to rely on the parish to support her family as she made an adequate living as a prostitute. She had already approached the local midwife to arrange for her care during her forthcoming confinement and, when the midwife asked her who the baby's father was, Elisabeth refused to name him, although she did say that he was a respectable man of considerable means, who had willingly agreed to pay her 2s a week to support his child.

On Saturday 21 July, Elisabeth left her children in her brother's care and went out to post a letter. Before she went out, she peeled some potatoes, asking her brother to put them on to boil ready for her return.

On her way, she stopped briefly at about nine o'clock in the evening to talk to two women, after which she apparently vanished into thin air. The potatoes were long since cooked and waiting for her, but she never came home to eat them.

Her family waited until darkness had fallen before going out to search for her. When they found no trace of her, they reported Elisabeth missing to the local police. However, given her lifestyle, it was believed that she was most probably with a 'gentleman friend' and would return in due course, undoubtedly with a little more money than she had left home with.

On the following morning, a collier noticed that the cabin doors of a coal pit were open. As he had checked and locked the doors on Saturday night and hidden the key, he went to investigate and found a number of items of women's clothing scattered around in the cabin and drag marks on the floor, leading to the mouth of the pit. Aware that Elisabeth Preece had been reported missing the previous night and had still not returned home, the collier immediately suspected that she might be in the pit. He alerted the authorities to his suspicions and, when a search was made, the dead body of Elisabeth was indeed found at the bottom of the pit, her head beaten to a bloody pulp and her face so injured that she was almost unrecognisable. Whoever had attacked Elisabeth had evidently found the concealed key to the cabin doors and perhaps persuaded her to go into the cabin to conduct their 'business' in relative privacy.

In the 1800s, there was no such thing as preservation of a crime scene and the gruesome discovery at the bottom of the coal pit brought a horde of curious villagers rushing to the site of the murder. Consequently, when the police began their investigations, there were very few clues to be found.

The nurse who washed and laid out Elisabeth's body noticed that the dead woman's chemise appeared to have been tucked into her stays 'as if by other hands than her own'. Elisabeth's clothes were torn and a pocket had been ripped clean away from her dress. The nurse also noticed the presence of marks on Elisabeth's breasts, which she was later to describe as 'something like finger marks.'

Two young boys came forward to say that they had been near the pit on Saturday night and had heard a woman's voice shouting 'Oh, Lord!' several times. The cries were initially very loud, then gradually faded in volume, as if the unfortunate woman were being strangled or suffocated.

The two young women with whom Elisabeth had talked on her way to post her letter told the police that they had seen a man nearby, leaning over a gate and watching them. They described him as wearing striped trousers and a dark velvet jacket and added that, when the man realised that they had seen him, he had skulked away along the hedge, turning his face away as if he didn't want to be recognised. A number of other people had seen what appeared to be the same man, although none of the villagers recognised him and nobody was able to name him.

An inquest was opened at the Nag's Head public house, before coroner Mr Joseph Dickens and amazingly, having heard all the evidence, sparse though it was, the jury seemed to be leaning towards a verdict of suicide. The attending police officers objected most strongly to this verdict, insisting that Elisabeth had been wilfully murdered and, in the end, the jury compromised with a verdict of 'Found dead', the equivalent of an open verdict, which would allow further enquiries to be made into the unfortunate woman's death.

Despite the best efforts of the police, nobody was ever charged with the murder of Elisabeth Preece. Looking back at the newspaper reports of the case, it seems likely that her killer was a local person, since he or she not only knew of the existence of the coal pit, but was also able to locate the hidden key. The fact that Elisabeth's pocket was ripped from her dress might suggest robbery as a motive for her murder. Yet her torn clothes, the presence of finger marks on her breasts and the rearrangement of her underclothes, 'as if by other hands than her own', suggests a sexual motive, particularly in view of Elisabeth's chosen 'profession'. And who was the father of her unborn child? Could it be that the birth of an illegitimate baby was about to cause embarrassment for a 'respectable' gentleman?

A postcard of Pontesbury police station. (Author's collection)

Or was the prospect of having to pay 2*s* a week for the maintenance of the child sufficient motive for someone to want Elisabeth dead?

None of these questions are likely to be answered now. However, the police felt very strongly at the time that several people in the small, close-knit village of Pontesbury knew something about the murder and chose not to come forward with what they knew. If this were the case, they probably took the secret of the identity of the murderer to the grave and thus, as far as the killing of Elisabeth Preece is concerned, somebody quite literally got away with murder.

8

'DID YOU EVER SEE ANYTHING BETWIXT HER AND ME?'

Nesscliffe, 1854

John and Mary Gittins and their children lived in a cottage at Nesscliffe. They shared their home with two lodgers, one of whom was a twenty-seven-year-old labourer, John Lloyd.

On 20 January 1854, Mary Gittins gave birth to a baby and, after her confinement, her husband temporarily moved out of the marital bedroom, sharing a room with John Lloyd for a few days to give her time to recover. On 27 January, John Gittins awoke at five o'clock in the morning to hear the new baby screaming loudly. Gittins dug the sleeping Lloyd in the ribs and told him, 'John Lloyd, you must get up and nurse your bastard.'

'What do you say?' asked Lloyd incredulously, unable to believe he had heard his landlord properly. Gittins repeated his words.

'Did you ever see anything betwixt her and me?' Lloyd asked him, to which Gittins muttered something unintelligible in reply.

The accusation against John Lloyd led to an argument between him and his landlord and landlady, after which Mary Gittins asked him to leave the house later that day. Lloyd agreed to do this, yet even in the difficult circumstances under which he was leaving, he and Gittins still appeared to part on friendly terms, with Lloyd asking Gittins before he left if he owed him anything.

Having returned to live at his father's house in the village, Lloyd made only one more visit to his former home to retrieve a scythe he had left there. Yet Gittins wouldn't leave him alone. At the beginning of February, he sought out Lloyd and told him that the new baby was a 'sour, pouch-mouthed thing, just like you.' Lloyd was furious and told Gittins that he would give him a 'damn good tanning' for scandalising him without cause, but Gittins fled before he had the chance to carry out his threat. Yet outwardly there still seemed to be no show of animosity between the two men. When the Gittins' house caught fire towards the end of February, their neighbours rallied to extinguish the flames and John Lloyd was among those helping.

On 28 February 1854, the Gittins' son, Henry, was at home from his job in service at Felton. He woke early and, at half-past five in the morning, went downstairs and sat in the chair by the fireplace. A few minutes later, his father also came downstairs and Henry vacated the chair to allow him to sit down and moved to stand by the window. John was bending down putting on his boots when there was a sudden crash of breaking glass and Henry felt something whistle through his hair.

Mary Gittins shouted from upstairs to ask Henry what he had broken. 'Nothing,' said Henry. He went to the door and looked outside, but it was dark and raining and he couldn't see anything so he went back indoors.

By now, Mary Gittins had run downstairs to see what was happening. As soon as she entered the kitchen, she could smell gunpowder and see faint wisps of smoke, but John assured her that he wasn't hurt. Within a few minutes, John Gittins walked back upstairs and lay down on his bed. Although he made no complaint, his head seemed to be hurting and Mary put a handkerchief on it, even though she could see no signs of any injury.

John lay down for about twenty minutes then got up and went downstairs again. Henry had left to return to his employment, so John Gittins lit the fire and put the kettle on. When Mary followed him downstairs, he was sitting in his chair. Only then did she notice some shots in the wall by the fireplace and realise that her husband had in fact been shot. She screamed loudly.

The noise attracted her neighbours, among them Robert Evans, the landlord of the Three Pigeons Inn at Nesscliffe and his employee, the Gittins' former lodger John Lloyd. Both ran towards the sound of the screams, with Lloyd reaching the Gittins' house first. He ran into the house then, within seconds, ran out again saying to Evans, 'Lord, master! Go and see what you can do. I can't go; they will think something of me.'

Evans went into the house and found John Gittins slumped in the corner in a faint. He sent for a doctor and the police then went back outside where he told John Lloyd, 'Lord bless me, Jack. Somebody's shot Gittins. It's a dreadful thing.'

'It is,' replied Lloyd.

'I daresay they will have suspicion on you,' continued Evans.

'I daresay they will, but thank God I was not there last night till near six o'clock this morning,' said Lloyd.

When the police arrived at the home of John Gittins, they found three small panes of the kitchen window broken, apparently by gunshot. Outside the house, there were traces of gunpowder on the remaining windowpanes and on the lead

The Three Pigeons Inn, Nesscliffe. (© N. Sly, 2008)

between them, which Superintendent Thomas Evans was able to wipe off with his finger. Inside the house, the wall by the fireplace was peppered with shot.

By now, there were a number of people milling around outside the cottage and Evans heard rumours that John Lloyd might have been involved in the shooting. He immediately went with constables Humphrey and May to Lloyd's father's home, where a shotgun was found in a pigsty. It had obviously been recently fired. In John Lloyd's bedroom the police found a jacket, the pockets of which contained some shot and a cartridge case, along with the bowl of a tobacco pipe, often used for measuring gunpowder.

The police went straight back to the Three Pigeons Inn, where they found John Lloyd working in a barn and immediately arrested him, charging him with shooting at John Gittins with intent to murder him. 'This is a damned calamity. There will be an end of me,' said Lloyd, as he was taken away for questioning.

Lloyd was asked to surrender his boots, which were then compared with footprints in the soft earth outside the kitchen window of the Gittins' house. They appeared to match exactly, even down to a bulge in one side of the left boot.

The charge against John Lloyd was amended to one of wilful murder after John Gittins died from his injuries in the Salop Infirmary on 10 March. Just two weeks later, Lloyd was tried at Shrewsbury before Mr Justice Wightman. Mr Huddleston and Mr Scotland prosecuted, while Mr Hodgson defended Lloyd.

The prosecution had commissioned carpenter Thomas Humphreys to make a model of the Gittins' cottage to demonstrate exactly from where the shot had been fired.

It was quickly established that the kitchen window was 4ft from the ground outside of the house and that the shooter had fired from an open space directly behind the kitchen, the shot hitting Gittins in the head as he bent to put on his boots.

The prosecution first called Mrs Gittins and then her children, Sarah, aged fifteen, and Henry, aged seventeen, to testify about the events of the early morning of 28 February. They then called a procession of witnesses who had spoken to John Lloyd after the shooting was discovered. These included Robert Evans and a labourer, John Jacks, who had been present when Lloyd was arrested and who told the court that Lloyd had remarked, 'I suppose some of you Nesscliffe gentlemen will come and see me when I am going to be hung.'

Another witness, William Evans, told the court that he had spoken to Lloyd a few weeks before John Gittins had been murdered. The two men had been drinking at the New Inn, Nesscliffe, when a half-drunk Lloyd had pulled a length of rope out of his pocket and tearfully said, 'This will be my doom before morning.' Evans again saw Lloyd on the night before the murder, carrying something under his left arm. It was dark at the time and although Evans couldn't swear to it, he believed that the object he had seen Lloyd carrying was a shotgun.

Evidence was given that Lloyd had borrowed a shotgun from a man called Dick Richards on the pretext of wanting to shoot pigeons. In the days immediately before the murder, he had set about obtaining shot, cartridge cases and gunpowder from a number of local sources. He had made no attempt to be secretive about readying the weapon for shooting, even asking people to obtain cartridges for him.

After hearing testimony from the three police officers who had been involved in the murder investigation and the arrest of John Lloyd, the prosecution rested.

Shrewsbury Royal Infirmary. (Author's collection)

The counsel for the defence had very little to say, beyond pointing out to the jury that most of the evidence against the prisoner was circumstantial. This was further emphasised by Mr Justice Wightman in his summing up of the case for the jury.

The judge told the jury that there was no argument about the fact that John Gittins had been shot in the head on 28 February. Several of the pellets had penetrated his brain, some to a depth of 3in, and this had been the cause of his death on 10 March. There was also no argument about the fact that the shooting had taken place between five and six o'clock in the morning. If the party who fired the gun did so wilfully with the intention of doing grievous bodily harm to the victim then the act would amount to murder. What the jury needed to decide, said the judge, was whether or not the prisoner was that man.

The judge asked the jury to consider whether Lloyd had a motive for committing the murder. Was the accusation of fathering a bastard child sufficient motive for him to kill the person who made it? Mr Justice Wightman reminded the jury that Lloyd had been seen coming from the direction of his own home at half past six on the morning of the murder. This could be taken as a sign of either innocence or guilt, he said. It could indicate that Lloyd had not left his home before that time, so could not have fired the shot that killed his former landlord. On the other hand, it could mean that Lloyd had fired the shot at half-past five then gone home to leave the shotgun.

Mr Justice Wightman concluded his summary by telling the jury that they must decide whether or not Lloyd fired the fatal shot and, if they believed that he had done, whether he had shot with intent to do grievous bodily harm or with the intent of frightening the victim. If they believed that there had been intent, then they must find Lloyd guilty but, if they had any reasonable doubt, then they must acquit him.

The jury retired for half an hour before returning a verdict of 'Guilty' against John Lloyd, who was immediately sentenced to death.

Once incarcerated in Shrewsbury Gaol, Lloyd made a full confession to the prison chaplain. He stated that he had been so angered by suggestions that he had been intimate with Mrs Gittins and that he was the father of her baby that he determined to get revenge for the false accusation. He had in fact made more than one attempt to kill John Gittins, before deliberately shooting him through his kitchen window. (Even then, he had almost failed in his quest for revenge, as the gun had misfired three times.)

On a previous occasion, he had intended to intercept John Gittins at the roadside and kill him with a hatchet. However, Gittins had failed to appear as expected. On that occasion, Lloyd actually approached another passer-by, mistakenly thinking that he was Gittins.

John Lloyd was hanged for the murder of John Gittins at Shrewsbury Gaol on 7 April 1854.

9

'DO YOU HEAR HOW THEY ARE QUARRELLING?'

Much Wenlock, 1857

Ann Morgan, otherwise known as Nancy Morgan or Ann Evans, was sixty-five years old and made her living as a fortune-teller in the area of Much Wenlock. Such was the gullibility of her clients that, over the years, she had amassed a tidy sum of money. Ann, who frequently spoke in tongues, was rumoured to practice witchcraft and to possess supernatural powers, including that of the 'evil eye'. In 1850, Ann's husband died and, within twelve months, Ann had found a new suitor, who promptly moved in to share her cottage on Westwood Common.

William Davies was described in the newspapers of the time as being of rather weak intellect. The fact that he was only in his mid-thirties and professed to love Ann Morgan very much was taken as evidence of this, particularly as the same newspapers described Ann as 'a disgusting old woman'. It was widely believed that Davies was lazy as well as stupid and that part of Ann Morgan's attraction was that her savings enabled him to live a life of idleness rather than having to work as a labourer. If this was indeed the case, then Davies must have been extremely lazy, since he was prepared to tolerate Ann Morgan's violent temper and foul mouth and to bear the almost constant verbal and physical abuse that she allegedly subjected him to.

On 12 September 1857, Ann sent William to Much Wenlock to do some shopping for her. When he took longer than she expected to return home, she set off in a temper to meet him, finding him walking homewards at the turnpike gate, just outside the town. In no uncertain terms, Ann told him what she thought of him, using a tirade of foul and abusive language that continued unabated long after the couple reached home.

Ann Rowlands, a near neighbour, professed herself to be shocked by the loud argument, saying that Ann Morgan was using 'such oaths that I never heard'. Mrs Rowlands asked another neighbour, Ann Edwards, 'Do you hear how they are quarrelling?' but Mrs Edwards had heard it all before. 'This is nothing. They will be great friends again shortly,' she reassured Mrs Rowlands. However, her words were soon proved wrong as, just a few minutes later, Mrs Rowlands's young son, John, came home and told his mother that Billy was killing Mrs Morgan.

Mrs Rowlands went directly to Ann Edwards's home and together the two women rather warily approached Ann Morgan's cottage. As they stood hesitantly on the threshold, a passing rag and bone man, William Matthews, heard them nervously calling out to Ann Morgan and came to see what the matter was.

Matthews opened the locked cottage door, using a spare key held by Mrs Rowlands, and went inside, closely followed by the two neighbours. As he opened the door, Matthews noticed that there was a spot of blood near the latch, as if it had been left there by a bloody finger or thumb and, when Mrs Rowlands investigated upstairs, she found the body of Ann Morgan stretched out on the floor of the landing, lying dead in a pool of blood.

The police and a doctor were called. When Mr William Penny Brookes, a surgeon from Much Wenlock, arrived he found that Ann Morgan's throat had been cut.

Much Wenlock, 1800.
(Author's collection)

43

He noticed a large amount of blood on the floor downstairs and noted that Ann had several other wounds to her face and neck. As well as some superficial wounds, these included an irregular cut on her left eyebrow which had gone right through to the bone beneath and four stab wounds on the back of her neck, each of which had penetrated to a depth of around 2in. Much of the interior of the cottage was liberally splattered with blood.

On the following day, coroner Mr E.G. Bartlam arrived to inspect the body and requested that Mr Penny Brookes and another surgeon, Mr James, conduct a post-mortem examination. The two surgeons found that two deep cuts behind Morgan's ear had penetrated the internal carotid artery, which would have caused massive blood loss and led to almost instantaneous death. At a subsequent inquest, held at a local hotel, the jury returned a verdict of wilful murder against William Davies.

Meanwhile, PCs Alder and Roberts had arrived at the cottage shortly after the discovery of the body and, having been told that William Davies had been seen calmly locking the door and walking away towards Lushcott, the two officers set off in pursuit. On reaching Lushcott, they were joined by farmer Mr Edward Cleeton, who offered to help with the search. They eventually reached Leasown Farm near Leebotwood, where Davies's father lived and were told by the farmer's wife, Mrs Cound, that William and his father had both gone out.

PC Roberts went on to the village public house in search of Davies, while PC Alder and Mr Cleeton waited at the farm in case he returned. At two o'clock in the morning, Davies was found, lying concealed with his father beneath some straw in a barn at the farm. PC Alder immediately arrested him and charged him with the murder of Ann Morgan.

'Is she dead?' asked Davies, and, when told that she was, replied, 'Oh, Lord. I did not think it was quite so bad as that.'

Taken to the lock-up at Much Wenlock, the police noticed that Davies's smock was stained with blood. Davies tried to explain this by saying that he had 'stuck a fowl' a couple of days earlier. He insisted on talking, even though the policemen cautioned him.

Davies maintained that Ann Morgan had sent him into Much Wenlock to do some shopping and that, while there, he had stopped for a drink at the pub. Davies insisted that he had used his own money to buy his drink, but when Ann Morgan met him on the road home, she had been equally certain that it had been bought with her money and was not happy. A furious Ann called him a 'damned liar' and a 'damned villain', accusing him of stealing her money to buy alcohol. Davies remained calm and, according to witnesses, walked quietly and civilly with Ann until they reached the cottage.

Once inside, it appears that Davies finally lost his temper. He threw some of the sugar he had just bought into the fire and told Ann that he was leaving, starting to collect his work clothes together in readiness to do so. He asked Ann Morgan to give him a silver watch that, according to Davies, she had previously given him as a gift. Morgan had refused and denied ever having given him the watch, which she

Much Wenlock's former police station. (© N. Sly, 2008)

said had belonged to her late husband. A ferocious dispute about the ownership of the watch followed – it was later found tightly clutched in Ann Morgan's hand, the chain wrapped around her fingers.

William Davies was brought before magistrates, charged with the murder of his common-law wife. The court heard evidence from the neighbours, including young John Rowlands, who was described as 'an intelligent little boy'. John told the court that he knew both Ann Morgan and William Davies well enough to recognise their voices – indeed, he referred to Ann as 'my aunt', although she was not related to him in any way.

John related that he had heard the couple quarrelling and Ann Morgan had said that if Davies didn't leave then she would make him go. John heard Davies climbing the cottage stairs, saying that he was going to fetch his work smock. Ann Morgan followed him, at which there was a loud thump as if she had been knocked down onto the floor. Ann then shouted, 'Leave me alone, Billy', after which she screamed loudly three times. Then things had gone ominously quiet for a few minutes, before John saw William Davies leaving the house, his face and smock covered in blood. John had asked Davies where he was going and Davies had replied, 'To the Knoll'.

Having heard evidence from Mr Penny Brookes, the surgeon, from the police officers and from Mr Cleeton, the court next heard from Mr Thomas Haynes, an ironmonger from Much Wenlock. Haynes identified a large, bloody clasp knife found on the dresser of Ann Morgan's cottage as one that he had sold to William Davies just two days before the murder.

Although he was not defended in court, Davies was given every opportunity to question the witnesses, a chance he largely declined, saying that the testimony did not make much difference to him. In the face of such apathy, it came as no surprise when he was committed to stand trial at the next Shropshire Assizes.

The trial opened in March 1858 before Mr Baron Watson. Mr Scotland and Mr Benson appeared for the prosecution, while, at the request of the judge, Mr Powell agreed to defend William Davies, assisted by Mr G. Brown.

Not one of the witnesses who appeared in court could find anything good to say about Ann Morgan. Many of them had feared her in life to the extent that some witnesses appeared to believe that Ann Morgan could still exercise her mystical powers against them from beyond the grave.

Mr Powell, for the defence, claimed that Ann Morgan had somehow bewitched William Davies into living with her and that, no matter how many times he tried to leave her, she always drew him back. According to Mr Powell, Davies had always born Ann Morgan's violence and abuse with great patience and quietness and he had absolutely no motive for murdering her. On the contrary, it was in his interest to keep her alive and ultimately marry her so that he might legitimately inherit her savings. Morgan had recently sold a plot of land and the proceeds from the sale had been placed in the bank. Although there was money in the house, as well as bankbooks, Davies had taken nothing with him when he left the cottage.

Powell theorised that Ann Morgan had probably attacked William Davies when he had tried to leave her, possibly attempting to use black magic in order to prevent him from going. Davies had not planned to kill Ann Morgan and for that reason alone, the counsel for the defence asked the jury to consider a reduction of the charge against him from murder to manslaughter.

The judge explained the difference between murder and manslaughter to the jury, saying that, before reaching a verdict, they should consider whether or not there had been any provocation by Ann Morgan. He reminded them that William Davies had said that there had been 'a scuffle', but that he had not specifically mentioned Ann Morgan striking any blows. As a deadly weapon had been used in the killing, the judge told the jury that the charge could only be reduced to manslaughter if they believed that Morgan had physically provoked Davies immediately before her death.

The jury considered this information before returning with a verdict of 'Guilty', leaving the judge no alternative but to pronounce sentence of death on William Davies.

His defence counsel immediately appealed this sentence, on the grounds of the provocation that Davies had suffered prior to murdering Ann Morgan. The appeal was upheld and, in April 1858, the death sentence against William Davies was commuted to one of penal servitude for life.

10

'WHAT HAVE YOU DONE WITH HIM?'

Baschurch, 1862

Edward Cooper had been happily married until his wife died, leaving him to bring up their two children alone. Although Cooper was a steady, hard-working man, his job as a farm labourer was poorly paid. Cooper needed to work in order to support his family, but, at the same time, his children were too young to be left to their own devices, particularly his son, John, who had been terribly injured when a door fell on him. As a consequence, eight-year-old John had a hunchback and a deformed chest and, although he was a clever little boy, he was not physically capable of working for a living, as many young children in the 1860s were expected to do.

The obvious answer to Edward Cooper's childcare problems was for him to find a new mother for the children and to that end he proposed to Jane Saddler, a servant at the farm next door to the one where he lived and worked. Jane turned him down flat after being informed by her employer, Mr Woolrych, that Cooper was not considered to be 'of good character'. Thus Cooper was forced to continue boarding his children out and, since he earned very little money, he soon fell behind on his payments to the families who had agreed to care for them.

It was for this reason that Cooper turned to Thomas Jones, a labourer from Baschurch. Cooper had known Jones and his wife, Sarah, for about six years and it was they who cared for his daughter, Jane. In December 1862, Edward Cooper arrived unexpectedly at the Jones's home, with young John in tow. Telling Thomas and Sarah that he had been trying to arrange for the children to be taken into the workhouse, Edward spent the night at their house. When he left the next morning, he conveniently 'forgot' to take John with him.

Baschurch. (© N. Sly, 2008)

Thomas and Sarah Jones kept young John for two or three days, clearly expecting his father to return for him. However, as well as being crippled, the Jones's soon noticed that John was covered with spots and appeared to be constantly scratching himself.

Eventually, a concerned Thomas Jones escorted the boy to the farm where his father worked, showed Edward the child's rash and demanded to know what was wrong with him. He made it quite clear to Edward Cooper that he was not prepared to let the child stay in his house any longer.

Cooper was distraught and begged Thomas to take the boy, saying that if he didn't then he would hang himself and his son that evening. In the face of such a threat, Jones relented and agreed to take the child home with him for the night to allow Edward time to make alternative arrangements for his care. However, he stressed to Cooper that he must collect his son the following morning, saying that if he didn't then he would have no hesitation in sending him back to his father. Perhaps not surprisingly, Cooper failed to arrive to collect the boy as agreed and, as he had threatened, Thomas Jones promptly turned him out of the house, getting his twelve-year-old daughter to escort the boy back to his father's place of employment.

Cooper's employer, William Lewis, was none too pleased to find that he had suddenly acquired an extra lodger, especially one who was physically incapable of doing any work around the farm. He allowed John Cooper to stay from 8-14 December, having informed Edward in no uncertain terms that the arrangement was not going to be a permanent one. Cooper assured his employer that he had arranged a suitable place for the boy. Father and son left the farm together on 14 December 1862 and Edward returned alone the next day. Chastised by Mrs Lewis for missing a day's work, Edward apologised and told her that he was now 'done with the boy forever'. Worriedly, Mrs Lewis asked, 'What have you done with him?' to which Cooper replied that he had sent his son to Manchester to live with his grandmother.

Cooper had indeed taken his son to a relative, his uncle from Great Hanwood, who was also called John Cooper. They had arrived on the evening of 14 December and Edward had asked if it would be possible for them to stay the night. They were given a bed but left together at just before seven o'clock on the following morning.

Edward and his son were next seen at the village blacksmith's shop where Cooper went to get a light for his pipe and to ask blacksmith Richard Littlejohn for directions to Baschurch. However, they obviously did not follow the directions that they were given as they were next seen off the footpath, heading towards the river. The next time Edward Cooper was sighted, he was alone.

Mary Abbot lived in World's End Cottages at Baschurch. On the afternoon of 15 December, Edward Cooper knocked on her door and asked her if he might borrow a spade, which he took away with him, returning it to its owner after about forty-five minutes.

Whitmore Lane, Baschurch, which was formerly known as World's End Lane. (© N. Sly, 2008)

Mary Abbot knew Cooper by sight and spoke to him about a month later, when she passed him at his work in the fields. Knowing that Cooper had a son, Mrs Abbot enquired about him and was told that he was in Liverpool with Cooper's mother.

Over the next couple of month's Cooper gave conflicting accounts of his son's whereabouts to several different people, but it was a casual conversation over a few drinks in the pub that really aroused people's suspicions about young John Cooper's wellbeing. Mr Abbot, from whose wife Edward Cooper had borrowed a spade, remarked that he was willing to bet that Cooper had used it to bury his son in a nearby ash coppice. The remark was brought to the attention of Sergeant Peter Bullock of the Baschurch Police, who took it upon himself to make some discreet enquiries about John. When there was no trace of the boy in Liverpool or Manchester, Sergeant Bullock and his colleague PC Robert Brookfield made a search of the ash coppice near to World's End, where they soon found a shallow grave containing the decomposing remains of a little boy with an unmistakeable hunchback.

The child's remains were taken to the nearby Duncan Inn, while Superintendent Joseph Ivens of the Oswestry Police went off in search of Edward Cooper. He found him ploughing a field and asked him where his son was. Cooper told the officer that he had sent the boy to live with his grandmother in Manchester, but Ivens told him that the boy was missing and that Cooper must accompany him to the police station to answer some questions. Having been officially cautioned, Edward Cooper then confessed that he had sold his son to a passing gypsy for half a crown.

Meanwhile, two Baschurch surgeons were carrying out a post-mortem examination of the child's body. They found that the organs had deteriorated too much for them to be able to state with any certainty whether or not the boy had died of natural causes, although the presence of a twisted white handkerchief, tied tightly in a double knot around the child's neck, made it seem most likely that he had been strangled. Both surgeons were familiar with John Cooper and, although his facial features had decomposed too badly for him to be recognisable, both men identified the boy's deformed back and chest.

As the last person to be seen with John Cooper, his father Edward was charged with his wilful murder and brought to trial at the Spring Assizes in Shrewsbury. The proceedings opened on 23 March, presided over by Mr Justice Crompton, with Mr Boughey and Mr Benson prosecuting, while Mr W.H. Cooke was requested by the judge to act in the prisoner's defence.

The prosecution opened the trial by calling a number of witnesses including Thomas and Sarah Jones, William Lewis and his wife, Mrs Abbot and Richard Littlejohn the blacksmith. William Hughes, who was acquainted with the Coopers, had seen Edward and John pass within 10 or 12 yards of his cottage on 15 December, Cooper tightly clutching his son's hand. John Walton, Thomas Thomas and William Diggory also testified. The three farm labourers had been working in the fields cutting turnip tops and had seen Edward Cooper leading his son towards the ash coppice where his body was found two months later. Yet more witnesses had seen Edward Cooper alone later that day.

The prosecution rested after hearing testimony from the investigating officers and the two surgeons who had examined the child's body and when the defence opened, it was the evidence of the two doctors that Mr Cooke immediately challenged.

'Was the dead body found in the ash coppice that of the prisoner's little boy?' he asked the court, pointing out that identification of the remains had been made by people who had barely known the child in life, while people like Sarah Jones, who had actually cared for the boy and must frequently have washed and dressed him, had not been called upon to view the body. On these grounds alone, argued the defence counsel, it would be unsafe to convict Edward Cooper of murdering his child when nobody could be completely sure that John Cooper was actually dead. Even if Edward Cooper had taken the boy to the coppice with the intention of murdering him, why would he have chosen such a public route, knowing that his movements would be likely to be observed? Edward Cooper, the defence maintained, was extremely familiar with the area and could easily have chosen a more private and secluded location, had he intended to kill his son.

The jury were not convinced by Mr Cooke's arguments and, after hearing the judge summarise the case, needed only a brief deliberation to find Edward Cooper 'Guilty' of the wilful murder of his son, John. Having listened to Mr Justice Crompton pronouncing the death sentence and advising him to hold out no hope of mercy, Cooper asked him, 'My Lord, may I speak?'

Given permission, Edward addressed Mr Woolrych, the farmer whose condemnation of his character had deterred his servant Jane Saddler from accepting Cooper's proposal of marriage. 'Mr Woolrych, you are a Christian gentleman,' said Cooper. 'It is you who brought me to the place of judgement; it is you and your servant Jane Saddler who bring me to the execution tree.' Whether or not Mr Woolrych or Jane Saddler made any response is not recorded but thirty-year-old Edward Cooper was hanged at Shrewsbury on 11 April 1863.

11

'ALL MUST DIE SOMETIME OR ANOTHER'

Longden, 1867

Christmas is supposed to be the season of peace on earth and goodwill to all men. However, in 1867, for one little girl there would be no festivities, no Christmas dinner or plum pudding, and no stocking on Christmas morning.

Nine-year-old Catherine Lewis, the oldest of five children, was the daughter of a labourer, Edward, who lived in Longden. On 22 December 1867, she left her parents' home intending to go to a neighbour's house where she could occasionally earn some pocket money as a babysitter. Having spent the day with Mrs Ann Davies, Catherine attended chapel in the evening, leaving to walk home in the company of two villagers, a woman named Jane Richards and a man named John Mapp. Mapp was described as being quite handsome in profile. However, his good looks were spoiled by the fact that he had a pronounced cast in his eyes and he also walked with a slight stoop, making him seem smaller than his given height of 5ft 6in. He also had a severe speech impediment.

Just outside the village, Jane Richards left Mapp and Catherine at Whitfield's Farm, where she was employed as a servant. Mapp continued to walk on towards the village with Catherine by his side. The fact that Catherine failed to return home that night didn't unduly alarm her parents, as, in the past, she had frequently spent the night with the Davies family.

On 23 December, John Mapp was at work in the fields at Whitefield's Farm in the company of a young boy named John Aston. Looking in the hedge for a stout stick to use as a whip, Aston happened to notice something pushed into a holly bush and, when he went to investigate more closely, he retrieved a small, black straw hat, trimmed with a purple ribbon, which was saturated with blood. He showed the hat to Mapp, telling him that, in his opinion, whoever had been wearing the hat had obviously been seriously injured, judging by the amount of blood on it.

Together Aston and Mapp made a half-hearted search of the ditches close to the holly bush where the hat had been found in case somebody was lying injured and in need of help. They found nothing, so Mapp instructed Aston to bury the hat and forget about it. Aston refused, so Mapp picked up the hat and stated that he would have the ribbon from it. Again, Aston protested and eventually the hat was placed on a roadside gatepost.

Shortly afterwards, a Mrs Mary Hartshorne walked passed the field and, seeing the hat, recognised it as the one she had seen Catherine Lewis wearing in chapel only the night before. She picked up the hat and took it to the Lewis's home. Mrs Lewis, Catherine's stepmother, fainted at the sight of it and a horrified Edward Lewis immediately set out to search for his daughter, while Mrs Hartshorne took the bloody hat to the house of the Longden police officer. On her way there, she met John Mapp who spotted the hat in her hand and, with tears in his eyes, remarked, 'That has come to send me back again'. He begged Mrs Hartshorne not to say anything against him to the police and, doubtless uneasy at his strange behaviour, she promised that she would not.

Before a search party could even be assembled, Edward Lewis had already found his daughter's body in the hayloft of a small cowshed, about half a mile from where her hat had been discovered. The child's throat had been cut, severing her windpipe, and her black shawl had been tightly pulled around her neck with 8in or so forcibly stuffed into her mouth. Her hands and legs were covered with scratches and she had several thorns sticking into her cheeks. Her clothes and hair were covered in dirt, leaves and thorns and her pinafore and underclothes were saturated with blood. Mr John Davies Harries, the surgeon from Shrewsbury who initially examined the child's body, believed that the filthy state of her clothes was due to the fact that she had been dragged face down across the fields for some distance. He attributed Catherine's death to blood loss and also suffocation, caused by her shawl being rammed into her mouth.

The police were called to the scene and after dealing with the recovery of Catherine's body, which was taken to the Tankerville Inn at Longden, PC Edward Jones wasted no time in going to find Mapp. As the last person to be seen with the victim, he was obviously a prime suspect, and Jones was also aware that Mapp had a history of attacks on women and had only recently returned to England having been sentenced to a period of transportation for raping a married woman in her sixties.

Mapp denied all knowledge of the murder, admitting that he had walked with Catherine from the chapel but insisting that he had turned off the road to Whitefield's Farm, leaving Catherine Lewis talking to Jane Richards. Police seized the clothes that Mapp had been wearing on the Sunday evening and, on closer examination, found spots of blood and marks on his corduroy trousers, which suggested that he had recently been kneeling down on wet ground. The lower parts of the trousers seemed to have been recently washed or wiped, while there were bloodstains on the right sleeve of Mapp's jacket, on his handkerchief and on a penknife found lying on his kitchen table. Most damning of all was a small, cheap brooch, which was found in his jacket pocket – when last seen the dead girl had been wearing it to pin her shawl closed. Mapp swore to the police that the brooch belonged to him.

Mapp's behaviour since the murder had aroused suspicion, not least his reaction to Catherine's hat being found and his remarks to Mary Hartshorne. However, it was his behaviour at work that had seemed most unusual.

On the morning after the murder, John Aston told the police that Mapp had seemed exceptionally nervous and was continually looking around, as though expecting someone or something to arrive. When Catherine's body had been found, there was very little blood on the cowshed floor. Given the nature of her injuries, it was suggested that she had been killed elsewhere and her body then moved to the shed. The police went back to where the hat had been found. It was in a field of stubble that was being ploughed and dressed with horse manure at the time of the murder. Mapp had been spreading the manure, choosing to continue doing so without pause during what should have been his lunch break and, when the police officers took a rake and carefully moved it, they found large amounts of blood on the ground and also a hairnet like the one that Catherine had been wearing at the time of her death. They were able to locate drag marks between the field and the cowshed but, once more, there was very little evidence of blood staining along the trail between the two locations.

Thus it occurred to the police that Mapp had killed Catherine Lewis in the field on Sunday night then returned to the scene on the following morning, when he had hidden her body. They immediately took possession of the clothes he had worn for work on the Monday, finding bloodstains on the trousers, waistcoat and jacket.

Mapp was charged with the wilful murder of Catherine Lewis and brought before magistrates at the earliest possible date after Christmas. Having heard statements from all of the key witnesses, the magistrates then invited Mapp to give his side of the story.

He first asked permission to examine the clothes he had been wearing on the day after the murder and vehemently denied that the stains pointed out to him were bloodstains. He explained the bloody handkerchief by saying that he had cut his hand a couple of weeks ago while picking turnips and had wrapped it in the handkerchief to try and staunch the bleeding. He told the magistrates that he had bought the brooch found in his pocket as he was coming home from chapel on the night of Catherine's disappearance. He had paid 3d or 4d for it from a man whose face he had not seen clearly in the dark and would not be able to recognise again. His knife had been left in his working trousers on Saturday night and he had worn his best clothes to attend chapel, so had no knife with him on the Sunday. As for his behaviour at work on Monday morning, he denied moving the body, saying that he had only been in the field for a minute or two when John Aston arrived.

In spite of his declarations of innocence, Mapp was committed to stand trial at the next Shrewsbury Assizes in March 1868. Sir Fitzroy Kelly presided, with Mr Boughey and Mr Warren acting for the prosecution and Mr Harrington defending.

Since being incarcerated awaiting his trial, Mapp had been surprisingly cheerful, with a voracious appetite for food. He certainly had no problems sleeping at nights and seemed completely untroubled by the diabolical crime he was said to have committed. As he stood in court to plead 'Not Guilty', it was noted that he had gained weight since his appearances at the magistrate's court.

The outcome of Mapp's trial was a foregone conclusion. The proceedings were marked by the presence of hordes of angry spectators, who seemed more than willing to spare the hangman a job and lynch John Mapp themselves. Mapp was described as a man who was 'extremely dull at learning', who struggled to master even the most routine tasks in his job as a farm labourer. His defence counsel focused on the fact that much of the evidence against him was circumstantial. Considering the nature of the victim's injuries, there was remarkably little blood on Mapp's clothes and it had been impossible to prove that this was even human blood. Mapp's severe speech impediment gave rise to the possibility that his statements to the police might have been misunderstood. There was, Mr Harrington pointed out, no motive for the murder and he reminded the jury that no footprints had been found at the scene of the crime, suggesting that this indicated that a man of 'a better class' than the accused had committed the murder, since Mapp habitually wore heavy working boots which should have left deep impressions on the muddy ground.

The jury gave only scant consideration to the defence arguments, barely deliberating before delivering their verdict of 'Guilty'. John Mapp had exhibited a detached coolness throughout the proceedings and showed no emotion of any kind as the judge passed sentence of death on him.

After his trial, Mapp continued to protest his innocence. However, as the date for his execution drew ever nearer, he gradually began to change his story. On 29 March, Mapp made a revised statement, in which he confessed to having murdered Catherine Lewis, insisting that he had never had any intention of raping her. Yet it wasn't until the eve of his execution that he finally made a full and detailed confession.

He related how he had walked home from chapel with Jane Richards and Catherine Lewis. After Jane Richards left them, he had tried to engage Catherine in conversation and had taken hold of her hand, at which she had begun to cry. She had broken free and tried to run away but he had caught up with her and asked her to allow him to 'do something to her'. Catherine had refused, threatening to tell her father. 'Well, if you tell your father I'll cut your throat,' he told the frightened child then proceeded to do just that.

Having cut the girl's throat, he had then stuffed her shawl into her mouth and dragged her by her right arm across the fields into the cowshed where her body was later found. According to Mapp, at this stage Catherine Lewis was still alive but, by the time he had reached the cowshed, she was dead.

In the days leading up to his death, Mapp had shown little concern for his circumstances, remarking when asked if he was afraid, 'All must die sometime or another.'

Mapp was visited by his elderly parents, both of whom were over seventy years old. His seven siblings also visited, as did Edward Lewis, the father of his victim. Mapp was said to be extremely moved by these visits. His execution on 9 April 1868 was the last public one to be held at Shrewsbury Gaol and a massive and hostile crowd assembled outside the gaol to see him hang.

Death did not come easily to thirty-six year-old Mapp. On the morning of his execution he ate a substantial breakfast and seemed in good spirits and willing to chat to warders. Hanged by William Calcraft, the knot in the noose shifted from below his left ear to the right-hand side of his neck. In all probability this meant that Mapp was strangled to death, evidenced by the fact that he struggled convulsively at the end of the rope for what must have seemed like an eternity to the watching crowd. Although Calcraft always maintained that Mapp's death was instant, other onlookers insisted that life was not extinct for at least ten minutes.

12

'YOU'LL FINISH ME JUST NOW'

Mardol, Shrewsbury, 1874

By 1874, Emma Marston had lived with labourer Henry Dorricott for two years, sharing a room conveniently located off a narrow passageway behind the King's Head public house in Mardol, Shrewsbury. It was a fiery relationship, with frequent arguments, usually fuelled by the couple's fondness for drink. Emma, in particular, was regularly thrown out of the King's Head for being disorderly.

On 14 September, Emma and Henry went out drinking as usual in the morning and, on their return home in the early afternoon, seemed to be on quite friendly terms. However, the couple's apparent bonhomie did not last long and by two o'clock, they were engaged in an argument of such ferocity and volume that somebody notified the police. PC France was sent to investigate the fracas and, as he approached the couple's room, James Newton, the pub landlord, beckoned him over.

Newton had heard Emma begging to be let out of the house and Henry refusing to release her and was concerned for Emma's safety. PC France stood in the passageway outside the room for a while, listening intently to the argument and, within minutes of his arrival, the quarrelling couple fell silent. France was well used to being called to domestic disputes between them and knew from experience that they invariably sorted out their differences when they sobered up. Hence, he left without intervening, although he did return some forty-five minutes later.

By this time, Emma was standing outside the room. A window was broken and Emma was sobbing quietly, wiping blood and tears from her face with her apron. Despite the presence of the policeman, Emma made no complaint to him and seemed to France to be trying to get back indoors, asking someone inside, 'come, unlock the door'. As the row seemed to have abated, the policeman felt justified in leaving.

The King's Head, Shrewsbury.
(Author's collection)

However, after PC France's departure, the row flared up again and continued for the remainder of the afternoon, with Emma being seen several times sobbing at the window. At one stage, she was heard to say, 'You'll finish me just now', to which Henry replied, 'I will before I have done with you.'

Another occupant of the building, Amelia Arrowsmith, had just returned home at eleven o'clock that night when she heard the unmistakeable sound of a person falling downstairs, followed shortly afterwards by moaning and cries for help. Amelia and other neighbours went to check on Emma Marston and found her lying in a crumpled heap at the foot of the stairs, claiming that, in trying to go upstairs, she had fallen backwards. There was no sign of Henry Dorricott and Emma was unable to stand without assistance, so her neighbours helped her into her bed. Once there, she showed them huge areas of blackened bruising on her thighs, although she did not say how they had been caused.

Amelia looked in on Emma the following morning, by which time Emma also had two black eyes. Henry was there and seemed very concerned about her, sending for chemist Thomas Andrews to attend to her. Andrews found Emma's thighs and breasts to be a blackened mass of bruises and also noticed her two black eyes. When Andrews asked Emma how she had come by her injuries she said nothing, although Henry immediately answered that she had fallen downstairs. Andrews told Henry that Emma was in a very bad state, at which Henry seemed troubled and even tearful.

Andrews sent round medicine for Emma, but her condition had not improved when he visited her again on the following morning. Once again, Andrews asked Emma what had caused her bruises and, once again, Henry told him that she had tumbled downstairs. Andrews turned to Emma for confirmation but she remained mute.

He advised Henry to call out the parish doctor, stressing the gravity of Emma's condition. However, Emma died on 19 September without the doctor ever having been summoned.

A post-mortem examination, carried out by Dr John Willett, catalogued a frightful array of injuries to Emma Marston's body. As well as her two black eyes,

A postcard of Shrewsbury, c. 1900. (Author's collection)

she had severe bruising to her breasts, back, hips, shins, thighs and buttocks. Her back was swollen and puffy, one hip was dislocated and her toes were almost black. Willett described Emma's thighs as 'pulpefied' and her skin as 'congested'. In his experience, such congestion of the skin occurred only as a result of serious accident, extreme violence or lightning strike.

When Willett opened the body, he found pus on the lining of Emma's belly, which was gangrenous. The thigh muscles were so badly damaged that they had begun to putrefy before Emma's death.

Willett recorded the cause of Emma Marston's death as inflammation and peritonitis arising from her injuries and went straight from the post-mortem to the room shared by Emma and Henry to examine the stairs.

He immediately expressed his doubts that a fall down such a short staircase could have been responsible for Emma's dreadful injuries. Had the staircase been straight, rather than curved, and had it been 15 or 20ft long, then it might have been possible, but in this instance, a person falling backwards down the stairs would simply fall a short distance against the wall, rather than plunging from top to bottom.

Willett felt it highly improbable that falling down this particular staircase could have been the cause of Emma's death. Rather he felt that her injuries had occurred as a result of heavy blows or kicks repeatedly falling on the same area of her body. If indeed Emma had been beaten to death, then there was really only one viable suspect – Henry Dorricott. At the inquest, held before coroner Mr Corbett Davies at the Britannia Hotel, the coroner's jury indicted him for wilful murder, a verdict that was later repeated at the magistrate's court.

Dorricott's trial for the wilful murder of Emma Marston opened at Shrewsbury in March 1875, before Mr Justice Quain, with Mr Boughey and Mr Underhill prosecuting and Mr Plowden defending.

The court heard from numerous neighbours and passers-by who had all heard the row raging from Emma and Henry's room throughout most of 14 September of the previous year. These witnesses included PC France, who told the court that it was not his place to forcibly enter the house unless cries of 'Murder' were heard. Although Emma had actually been seen several times during the altercation, none of the witnesses could truthfully claim to have seen Henry Dorricott and, even though they had clearly heard a man's voice, not all of those who had heard the argument recognised it as Dorricott's voice. And, of course, nobody had seen Henry Dorriott actually inflicting any blows on Emma Marston.

After Emma had received her injuries, many of her neighbours had visited her and helped with her care. One, Mary Ann Ledbury, had helped to poultice Emma's bruised chest and another, Mrs Annie Eliza Allman, had sat with her at Dorricott's request for several hours while he had gone out. During the time she stayed with Emma, Mrs Allman had even rubbed her thighs with the lotion prescribed by Mr Andrews, the chemist. Despite this close contact with her neighbours, at a time when her alleged attacker was not present, it seemed that Emma had deliberately chosen not to reveal how she had really come by her terrible injuries, although even if she had, the rules regarding hearsay evidence would have prevented the witnesses from testifying on the subject.

Shrewsbury. (Author's collection)

Only one witness, Emma Jones, hinted at a conversation with Emma about the true nature of her injuries but, when she tried to relate this conversation in court, the counsel for the prosecution objected. The conversation was immediately ruled inadmissible and Mrs Jones was forbidden to repeat it, forced to confine herself to detailing only what she had actually seen.

In spite of Dorricott having called Emma a cow, a cat and a sow just hours earlier, not to mention many other choice names that the witnesses felt were too base to repeat in court, most of those witnesses stated that Henry was both loving and tender towards Emma after she took to her bed, saying that he seemed terribly upset by her injuries and that he had nursed her devotedly.

After the neighbours had testified, Mr Andrews and Dr Willett were called to the witness box; Andrews to relate his treatment of Emma Marston before her death and Willett to tell the court of his findings afterwards. After hearing from the medical witnesses, the prosecution rested.

For the defence, Mr Plowden stressed the point that nobody had actually seen Henry Dorricott in the house – they had merely heard the argument between Emma and a man and assumed he was there. Such rows were commonplace in the area and nobody had thought to intervene, not even the police officer – surely someone would have done something if they truly believed at the time that Emma was being murdered?

Emma was known to be a habitual drunkard and to have been drinking on the morning of 14 September. The stairs at her home were twisting and narrow and had no handrail. They were so poor that anyone, especially a drunken woman, might fall down them and cause such injuries as those from which Emma died. Besides, Amelia Arrowsmith had definitely heard somebody falling downstairs and Emma had said herself that she had fallen.

Finally, Mr Plowden beseeched the jury to ask themselves what was the motive for Emma's murder? The couple had lived together for some time and witnesses had testified in court how Dorricott had seemed distraught and nursed her tenderly 'after her fall.' Yes, the defendant and Emma did fight, admitted Plowden, but there was nothing to suggest that Dorricott wanted his partner dead.

After the judge had summed up the evidence for the jurors, they retired for two and a half hours before returning to say that, while they found that Emma Marston's death had been caused by the prisoner's violence, it was without any premeditation on his part.

The judge told them that he could not accept such a verdict and directed them that if they understood the term premeditation to mean prior planning or preparation to kill then they should be advised that this was not a prerequisite of murder. If their opinion were that the prisoner had inflicted grievous or dangerous bodily harm on the victim, such that would probably lead to her death and did in fact ultimately prove fatal, then that would be wilful murder. Intent to kill, even if it only arose at the very moment preceding death, was sufficient grounds for wilful murder, as was inflicting the injuries without caring whether the victim lived or died.

On the other hand, if the blows were only slight and death ensued, then the crime would be manslaughter. It would also be manslaughter if there had been any provocation or if the blows were given in hot blood.

The jury retired again, this time returning in a few minutes with a verdict of 'Guilty of wilful murder', but recommending mercy for the prisoner. The judge asked them on what grounds they made this recommendation and the jury replied that they did not think the accused intended to murder the deceased.

By now, the judge was bristling with exasperation. 'And you still find him guilty of murder?' he asked incredulously. He then explained once more that if the jury believed that Dorricott violently attacked Emma Marston not intending to kill her, but she subsequently died from her injuries, then it was clearly a case of manslaughter.

The jury retired to the deliberation room for the third time before finally returning with a verdict that appeared to satisfy the judge, finding Henry Dorricott 'Guilty of manslaughter'.

Mr Justice Quain then addressed Henry Dorricott. Telling him that he believed that the jury had taken an extremely humane view of the case, the judge then revealed to the jury for the first time that Dorricott had an extensive criminal record and, over the past sixteen years, had been convicted no less than eleven times of deeds of violence. Now he had kicked a woman to death.

In view of his criminal career, Mr Justice Quain believed that Dorricott deserved a severe punishment and he was therefore sentencing him to fifteen years of penal servitude.

It almost appears as if the judge believed that Henry Dorricott should be punished more for his record of previous convictions than for Emma's killing – in other words, his sentence was meted out because he was a bad man, rather than because he had viciously killed a woman with his feet and fists. As in the majority of cases of domestic abuse, his violence towards his partner, which ultimately led to her untimely death, took place behind closed doors with no witnesses. Thus, all of the evidence against Dorricott was circumstantial and it was probably this fact alone that saved him from a verdict of wilful murder, resulting in his own death by judicial hanging.

It is said that the average female victim of domestic abuse will tolerate seven incidences of violence against her before finally leaving her abusive partner. Reading accounts of this case, one wonders how many times Emma had been beaten before and, if she had survived this attack, would she have found the courage and strength to leave her abuser?

[Note: In the contemporary newspaper accounts of the case, there seems to be some discrepancy about the identity of the judge who presided over Dorricott's trial at the assizes. He is alternately named as Baron Huddleston, although Mr Justice Quain is the most frequently cited name.]

13

'OH, LAWS, SALLY, HE'S STABBED ME'

The biggest problem with living next door to your boyfriend or girlfriend is that he or she is extremely difficult to avoid in the event of a break up of the relationship. This was the case for twenty-four-year-old George Holmes, of Tinker's Lane, Market Drayton. George had been walking out with Esther Beech, the stepdaughter of his next-door neighbour, Mr Hopwood, for eighteen months. The couple were engaged and George fully expected the relationship to eventually lead to marriage.

Without warning – and, George felt, without reason – Esther suddenly broke off their engagement at the end of November 1877. Soon, she was seeing another man, twenty-two-year-old John Chidlow, a soldier in the 43rd Foot Regiment, and apparently telling him all sorts of stories about how George frequently got drunk and used to knock her about.

George's emotions went from hurt and confusion to anger and bitterness at being thrown over for another man by Esther and, on 22 December 1877, having seen Esther and John passing by his window arm in arm, he decided to confront her once and for all about the end of their relationship.

He knocked on Esther's door and demanded to be let in. Realising that George had been drinking, Esther initially refused him admittance, but George was insistent, telling her that he only wanted to see John Barnett, a friend who was currently inside the house. Eventually, Esther relented and let him in, but, when it became obvious that it was her George had really come to see rather than Barnett, she ordered him to leave. Barnett meanwhile had walked out of the room as soon as Holmes entered, sensing that there was going to be an argument and wishing to avoid any unpleasantness.

George wasn't about to take any orders from Esther. Telling her angrily to sit down, he slapped her hard across the face, causing her nose to bleed. Stunned, Esther fell back into a chair and John Chidlow jumped up to defend her. Sarah Lovatt, who lodged with Esther, bravely seized George's arms from behind and shouted at him to 'Stop that'.

As she hung onto George Holmes, Sarah Lovatt suddenly felt him slumping forward slightly and heard him saying, 'Oh, laws, Sally, he's stabbed me'. Seeing blood pouring from Holmes's chest, Sarah Lovatt screamed loudly, releasing her hold on Homes who staggered across the room to lean on the dresser. Hearing the commotion, John Barnett ran back into the room, while John Chidlow ran out of the house, slamming the door behind him.

Holmes was now on the point of collapse and Barnett moved swiftly across the room, managing to catch him before he hit the floor. Barnett then helped the injured man back to his own house. As they slowly walked the short distance, with Barnett supporting Holmes, Holmes told Barnett, 'Oh, laws, he has stabbed me and I would not have served him like that.' Although Chidlow's name was not mentioned, Barnett assumed that the 'he' Holmes referred to was his love rival.

Quite by chance, PC Banks, who lived in Tinker's Lane, was returning home from his shift as Barnett escorted the bleeding Holmes home. Just minutes earlier, Banks had encountered John Chidlow running past him on Stafford Street. Now he asked Barnett what had happened.

'Chidlow has stabbed me,' replied Holmes.

Banks immediately returned to the police station to report the incident. Esther Beech had already summoned a doctor to attend to George Holmes, so PC Lewis was despatched to find and talk to John Chidlow.

The doctor called by Esther, Dr Beales, found that Holmes had a single deep stab wound in his breast, which was bleeding heavily. Beales stitched up the wound as best he could, leaving Holmes to rest in bed. Meanwhile, PC Lewis was keeping watch at the home of John Chidlow's father and, at a quarter to seven the next morning, he saw Chidlow arriving at the house.

Chidlow saw Lewis approaching and before the constable got a chance to speak to the young man, Chidlow whipped off his topcoat and ran. Vaulting the garden fence, he raced across fields and eventually escaped the police pursuit by diving fully clothed into the River Tern, emerging a short while later when the coast was clear. A knife was later found on the route of Chidlow's flight from the police, although ownership was never positively traced to John Chidlow, who insisted throughout that he didn't possess a knife and hadn't for some time.

Chidlow next appeared on the doorstep of a friend, Hannah Hammonds, an hour after he had first fled the police from his father's home. Sopping wet and freezing cold, he told Hannah that the police were after him for stabbing 'Nowpy', as George Holmes was nicknamed. Tearfully, he swore to her that he had no knife, so could not have stabbed Holmes. Hannah felt sorry for the pitiful young man and took him into her house, drying him off and putting him to bed in

Market Drayton, c. 1900. (Author's collection)

her son's bedroom. The police tracked him there later that day but, when officers knocked on Hannah's door, she insisted that Chidlow was not there. (She was later to say that the officers were in plain clothes and hadn't identified themselves as policemen.) Chidlow heard the conversation between the two policemen and Hannah Hammonds and called downstairs. The police went straight up to talk to him and immediately arrested him for the attack on Holmes.

Over the next few days, it became apparent that medically George Holmes was going rapidly downhill. Such was the concern for his condition that, on 28 December, a magistrate was called to his home to take his deposition. It read:

> I remember on Saturday night the 22nd of December, between eleven and twelve o'clock on that night I was in Hopwood's house. Chidlow was there. I don't know that I spoke a word to him. I spoke to Esther Hopwood [Beech] and she ordered me out of the house. Chidlow took something out of his pocket and stabbed me. I said 'Chidlow has stabbed me.'

In the event, George 'Nowpy' Holmes lingered until 8 January 1878 before finally succumbing to his injuries. A post-mortem examination was carried out by surgeon Mr Meek, who found that the knife had penetrated the victim's chest to a depth of 4in, damaging the right lung. Consequently the lung had become inflamed and had begun to decompose near the site of the stab wound. Initially, the attack had sent George Holmes into shock and the damage to his lung had interfered with his ability to breathe, causing exhaustion. Finally, pleurisy had set in and it was that which had ultimately caused Holmes's death. Now the charge against John Chidlow was elevated to one of wilful murder.

An inquest was held at the Lamb Inn, Market Drayton, before coroner Mr Robert Temple Wright. The coroner's jury returned a verdict of wilful murder against John Chidlow, who was taken to Shrewsbury Gaol to await an appearance before the magistrates.

Unfortunately, as a result of a clerical mix up, the governor of Shrewsbury Gaol did not receive the appropriate paperwork to allow Chidlow to attend the magistrate's court in Market Drayton. Instead, the magistrates were forced to travel to the prison and conduct their hearing there, which left Chidlow without representation from his defence lawyer. He was offered the services of a local lawyer but declined, saying that he preferred to question the witnesses himself.

All of the witnesses from the inquest testified, all having made the journey from Market Drayton in order to do so. Once all their evidence had been heard, Chidlow asked if he might make a statement.

No doubt aware that Chidlow was not at that moment represented by counsel, the magistrates cautioned him against saying anything that might be used to his detriment at any future trial. However, despite the warnings from the magistrates, it seemed as if Chidlow was determined to have his say.

He related having been out with Esther on 22 December and her telling him that George used to get drunk and knock her about. As he walked her home, Esther had told Chidlow that George would probably come to her house drunk that very night. Because of this, Chidlow had been anxious to go home, but Esther had eventually persuaded him to come into the house with her.

They had been at home for about twenty minutes when Holmes arrived and, the minute he entered the house, George began to call Esther 'everything that was dirty' before hitting her on the nose. Seeing Chidlow, George had referred to him as Esther's 'fancy man' and had lashed out at him, knocking his cap off. A few minutes later, said Chidlow, he had seen a knife being passed under the table. When he last saw it, it was in Esther Beech's hand.

Chidlow insisted that he had run out of the house, wanting to avoid any trouble, but had heard Holmes complaining of being stabbed just as he was leaving. As he ran towards his home, Chidlow maintained that he had stopped a passing policeman and reported the argument at Esther's home to him.

On his way home, Chidlow had passed a farm where he had spotted some rabbit snares. He had taken three rabbits from the traps, concealing two inside his coat and one down his trousers. Immediately afterwards he had heard somebody crawling through a hedge and, believing it to be policemen, had run away. He had given his pursuers the slip but, when he arrived home, his father had opened the window and called to him, 'The bobbies are after you, Jack, for stabbing Nowpy Holmes.'

Chidlow had run from the police only because he believed that they had chased him from the farm where he had stolen the rabbits. He had thrown away the rabbits as he ran, eventually deciding to go to Mrs Hammond's house, where he was later arrested.

The magistrates were not convinced by his speech and committed him to stand trial at the Winter Assizes.

Since the assizes were already in progress, Chidlow's trial took place with almost indecent haste, opening at Stafford on 29 January before Mr Justice Lush. The case for the prosecution was handled by Mr Underhill and Mr Darling, with Mr Plowden defending.

Esther Beech told the court that the only thing that she could really remember of the night of 22 December was Holmes's arrival at her home and being struck by him on her face. The blow had stunned her and the next thing she knew was Holmes saying that someone had stabbed him. She denied scuffling with Holmes and had not seen him being stabbed. She could only recall Holmes and Sarah Lovatt being in the room when she first noticed that her former boyfriend was injured. Esther also told the court that, three weeks before Holmes's death, she had seen a pocket-knife in John Chidlow's possession.

Sarah Lovatt had been behind Holmes pinioning his arms, so had seen nothing, neither had she heard any cross words between Chidlow and Holmes prior to the stabbing.

Barnett had not been in the room at the time, only returning when Sarah Lovatt had screamed.

The policemen gave evidence about the pursuit and eventual capture of John Chidlow, and Hannah Hammonds and her son, William, told the court about the defendant's arrival on their doorstep.

The court then heard from Dr Beales who, since surgeon Mr Meek was unwell, was also permitted to read out his colleague's conclusions, drawn from the post-mortem examination of George Holmes.

The only major difference between the proceedings at the Assize Court and the Magistrate's Court was the reading of George Holmes's deposition.

Mr Plowden, for the defence, felt that there were enough contradictions in the story of the stabbing of George Holmes to raise doubts in the minds of the jury as to the identity of the murderer. If the witness statements were to be believed, only Esther Beech or John Chidlow could have inflicted the fatal wound and Chidlow denied owning a knife, but stated that he had seen one in Esther's hand shortly before the stabbing occurred. Even if Chidlow had inflicted the wound, he had done so after witnessing the victim striking his girl and hearing her called 'everything that was dirty'. This was provocation enough to momentarily deprive the accused of his normal state of reason and, because of this, the charge should be reduced from wilful murder to manslaughter. The stabbing of George Holmes, maintained Plowden, was a true crime of passion.

Mr Justice Lush then summed up the case for the jury, paying particular attention to the law regarding provocation. The striking of a man's wife was considered sufficient provocation to the husband to reduce the crime from murder to manslaughter, if the husband then killed the aggressor in hot blood. If the jury believed that the relationship between Chidlow and Esther Beech constituted that of man and wife, then the outrage he had witnessed would naturally arouse his passion. If he had inflicted the wound in question in passion, before his blood had time to cool, then the correct verdict would be guilty of manslaughter rather than murder.

It took the jury just three minutes to return with a verdict of 'Guilty of manslaughter' against John Chidlow, after which the judge addressed the prisoner.

Telling Chidlow that he believed the jury had found 'a very proper verdict', Mr Justice Lush told Chidlow that his life had only been saved because of the provocation he had received. However, that provocation was not enough to mitigate the punishment and, as the crime he had committed was next to murder then the judge felt bound to regard it as deserving the next degree of punishment to that of death. He then sentenced John Chidlow to penal servitude for life.

[Note: In various contemporary accounts of the killing, John Chidlow is referred to as John Childow. (Census records seem to support the former version.) Esther Beech is alternatively called Esther Hopwood – the surname of her stepfather, with whom she lived.]

14

'BOTH ME AND MY HUSBAND ARE FREE OF MURDER'

Kynnersley, 1883

On 9 February 1883, Joseph Bates, a gasman employed at Apley Castle, took an early morning walk around the banks of Apley Pool, looking for duck eggs. His dog was with him and the animal suddenly began to show a great deal of excitement, barking at something in the reeds surrounding the lake. Bates went to look more closely and spotted a bundle, tied up with green baize string. He retrieved the package and curiously unwrapped it, untying the string and peeling back a layer of paper to find a canvas-wrapped parcel, tied this time with black string. Having removed the string, Bates recoiled in shock as the canvas fell back to reveal the severed head of a little girl, aged around twelve years old.

He took his gruesome find straight to the police station at nearby Wellington where the immediate priority was to identify the deceased child. The police organised a search of Apley Pool, which was partially drained. On 13 February, the receding water revealed a second parcel, also wrapped in brown paper and tied with string. When the paper was removed, there was a calico bag beneath, in which was contained a pair of legs. Obviously belonging to a child, the legs had been roughly sawn at mid thigh. There was a wound on one of the big toes and a small area of skin missing from one heel.

The remains of the child were taken to Dr Brookes, who subjected them to a detailed examination. The head, which had been severed between the third and fourth vertebrae, was in a mummified state, the skin much darkened and decomposition was already well advanced. Brookes believed that the head had

A postcard of the River Severn at Atcham, 1920s. (Author's collection)

either been partly boiled or exposed to some kind of dry heat. He found evidence of numerous injuries that suggested that the dark-haired little girl had been killed by violence before dismemberment. The legs were definitely a pair and it was reasonable to assume that they belonged with the head and had therefore come from the same victim.

In spite of the decomposition, several people who viewed the head believed it to be that of Mary Elizabeth Mayo, otherwise known as Polly. Polly's family had moved to Kynnersley from Shrewsbury on 28 December 1882, after Thomas Mayo had been offered a position as a groom, working for Mr Ogle. When he moved to Kynnersley, Thomas had brought with him his wife, Eliza, and four children – two named William, Mary Elizabeth, and Annie. Thomas and Eliza had no children together, but both had been married before. Eliza had given birth to two sons during a previous marriage, including one of the boys called William, both of whom were later to be adopted by their grandmother. The other children in the Mayo household were three of five sired by Thomas in a former marriage and, to them, Eliza proved to be the kind of wicked stepmother normally only read about in fairy tales.

Neighbours of the Mayo's previous home in New Street, Shrewbury had reported the couple to the police several times after incidences of cruelty to the children, particularly Mary Elizabeth who was, according to her stepmother, a 'very naughty child'. On one occasion, Eliza had ordered one of her stepdaughters to strip naked, then flayed the child's bare back with a belt until it was covered with striped bruises. A surgeon who had subsequently examined the child had counted ten cuts where the edge of the strap had broken the child's skin. Eliza Mayo was prosecuted for this offence and sentenced to six weeks imprisonment with hard labour at Shrewsbury Gaol. On the same day as Eliza had thrashed the child, Thomas Mayo had apparently also beaten the same little girl with his belt. Brought before magistrates to give evidence, the child assured them that the beating hadn't hurt her as much as the one previously administered by her stepmother, since she had been allowed to keep her clothes on. Hence Thomas got away lightly and was not charged, but he was later to serve twenty-one days in prison with hard labour for having cruelly punished another of the children. Released from custody, he had found himself out of work and had been forced to move away from Shrewsbury to find a job.

Things did not improve for the children after the move to Kynnersley and, on 10 January 1883, a desperate Polly Mayo had run away from home. She got as far as Wall, near Kynnersley, appearing on the doorstep of Mrs Elizabeth Hughes cold, extremely dirty and half starved. The child had two black eyes, a bruised cheek and a recent scab on her face. Mrs Hughes took the frightened little girl into her house, put her by the fire to warm herself and made her some food, which Polly gobbled ravenously.

Mrs Hughes then called in her neighbour, Harriet Thomson to look at the child. Harriet peeled back Polly's filthy clothes to find an even filthier body, which she later described as being 'just skin and bone'.

Three hours after Polly had sought refuge with Mrs Hughes her stepmother appeared in Wall looking for her and was directed to Elizabeth's house by Harriet Thomson. Eliza immediately asked Polly who had brought her so far from home, but the frightened child made no reply. Elizabeth Hughes remonstrated with Eliza about the state of the child, telling her that Polly had said that Eliza was responsible for causing her black eyes. Eliza replied that the child 'told stories' and that she had received the black eyes in a childish fight with a playmate. Elizabeth looked to Polly for confirmation, but she appeared too frightened to speak. Eliza seized the child's arm and told her that she was a very naughty girl and that, if she continued to be so naughty, she would put her in the brook. At that, she dragged the silent child away and Elizabeth Hughes saw nothing more of her until she viewed the severed head at the police station some weeks later and identified it as that of Mary Elizabeth Mayo.

Tragically, Polly's one attempt to escape the cruelty she constantly suffered at home had been unsuccessful.

After the discovery of the child's body parts and the suggestions received by the police that they might be the remains of Polly Mayo, the police went to the Mayo's house on 12 February to interview her parents. There Eliza told them that Polly, who was actually ten years old, was living with her uncle, James Mayo, at Yockleton. The police went to find Thomas Mayo, who was working in the cottage garden. Asked where Polly was, Thomas told a different story, saying that his wife had taken his daughter to Shrewsbury to meet a cousin who was going to take the child to America.

In view of the couple's conflicting stories about the whereabouts of their daughter, Sergeant James Lloyd told Thomas Mayo that he was going to arrest him and cautioned him. 'I shall say nothing,' was Mayo's response and he then asked Sergeant Lloyd, 'Are you going to take my wife?' Lloyd said that he was.

Told that her husband had been arrested and charged with Polly's murder, Eliza Mayo was dismissive. 'Oh, he loves his children too well to murder them,' she told the police, insisting that, 'They are all right with their friends.'

With Mr and Mrs Mayo secured in the lock-up at Wellington and their remaining children taken into the workhouse, the police spent the next couple of days searching the Mayo's cottage. Neighbours had told them that the chimney had caught fire on the day after the child's head had been found, producing a foul stench, so the police raked through the ashes in the fireplace removing several fragments of bone. Unfortunately, at that time, it was impossible to determine whether the bones were human or animal, but the police did take away many other samples, which were sent to public analyst Thomas Porter Blunt. Blunt found spots and smears of blood on several articles taken from the house, including a patchwork quilt, some children's clothes, a blanket and a woman's dress. Blunt was able to state that all the bloodstains were 'mammalian' but could not specifically state that they were human. The police also found splashes and spatters of blood on the stairs, walls and doors of the cottage.

When police questioned the Mayo's neighbours, they discovered that Eliza Mayo had told them that she intended to take Polly to see a doctor at Shrewsbury, as the child had been complaining of feeling ill. Eliza had told one neighbour, Mary Evans, that she would have to start the long walk early as Polly was suffering from chilblains and had difficulty walking.

Other neighbours had heard different accounts. One, letter carrier John Ruscoe, told the police that he had met Eliza on the road to Shrewsbury on Saturday 3 February. Eliza had been carrying a large, obviously heavy, basket, the contents of which were covered with a cloth. Eliza had asked the postman if he had seen Polly, claiming to have lost her at the bottom of Apley Lane, having left her waiting there while she returned home to fetch her purse, which she had accidentally left on the kitchen table. Ruscoe told her that he had not come that way, at which Eliza bade him 'Good morning' and continued on her way.

Thomas Porter Blunt. (Courtesy of the Thomas Porter Blunt website)

The police came to the conclusion that one or both of her parents had killed Mary Elizabeth Mayo on the morning of 1 February and that her body had then been dismembered and the pieces disposed of on or around 3 February.

Both Thomas and Eliza eventually made statements to the police about the death of their daughter. Thomas told them that Eliza had led him a very unhappy life since their marriage and that the couple had often fallen out over her ill treatment of the children, particularly Polly and one of Eliza's own sons, William. 'I never hurt my child in her lifetime, nor caused her death,' Thomas continued.

According to Thomas, he had come home from work for his dinner to find Eliza upstairs. She had called to Thomas to join her and, when he did, he found Polly lying on the bed, obviously near to death. Eliza had told him that the child had fallen down in a fit. Thomas told the police that he had suggested going to fetch a doctor but that Eliza had prevented him from doing so. Thomas had then returned to his work for the afternoon, leaving Eliza tending to Polly. By the time he returned that evening, Polly was dead.

Eliza's statement was somewhat different. Her statement opened with the words, 'I want to tell you all as I have told Jesus.' According to Eliza, on 1 February, Polly had been perfectly healthy and making no complaints when she had suddenly fallen in a fit. Thomas had carried Polly to the bath to try and revive her and, while Eliza 'rubbed the dear child' he had gone to summon a doctor. However, the doctor was not at home, besides which Thomas had no money with which to pay him, so he had returned home again.

Polly had died soon afterwards, and Eliza had wrapped her body in a blanket. Both parents had kissed her fondly then the body had been placed in a box until the following evening, when Thomas had cut the child's body into pieces and parcelled them up so that they could be disposed of more easily. On the following day, Eliza had taken the body to Shrewsbury, dropping the trunk and arms in the river near Atcham Bridge and throwing the head and legs into Apley Pool. Police dragged a large section of the river close to Atcham Bridge, but never recovered any more parts of the body of Polly Mayo.

Eliza admitted to being guilty of concealing the death of her child but swore to the police; 'Both me and my husband are free of murder'. [*sic*]

Thomas and Eliza Mayo appeared at magistrate's court, charged with the murder of their daughter. Thomas was additionally charged with being an accessory to the murder. Although the couple weren't defended at the magistrate's court, they were permitted to question the witnesses and, during the course of the hearing, they argued with many of the witnesses, accusing them of lying or being 'in beer'. Nevertheless, they were committed to stand trial at the next assizes.

As soon as the Mayo's were placed together in the dock, they began a loud, animated conversation between themselves, forcing the court officials to call for 'Order'. They eventually quietened down sufficiently to plead 'Not Guilty' to all the charges against them. By now, a defence team had been appointed by the court to act for them.

The prosecution team of Mr Rose and Mr Bather called a steady stream of witnesses who testified to the cruel treatment of their children by both defendants. Then, after hearing from the many police officers involved in the investigation, Dr Brookes and Dr G. Hollis who had examined the child's remains, and analyst Thomas Porter Blunt, the prosecution called their star witness, thirteen-year-old William Mayo, Polly's older brother.

Dressed in his workhouse uniform, after first assuring the court that he knew where he would go if he told lies, William testified that he had last seen Polly sitting on the screen by the kitchen fire. He had not seen Polly fall down in a fit and had been told by his mother that, if anyone asked after his sister, he was to say that she had been 'sent off dressed up'. William said that he had seen his mother take a big pot of water upstairs and that, later that day, when his father came home for dinner, Thomas had wanted to send for a doctor, but Eliza would not allow him to go.

William told of moving to Kynnersley and of his stepbrother – the other William – being sent away after about two weeks. He then confirmed much of the testimony of the Mayo's neighbours. He recalled the chimney catching fire, saying that his mother had been burning a lot of straw beforehand and the blaze had got out of hand. He told the court that his father had also spoken to him about Polly and told him what to say if he was asked any questions, which was that Polly had dropped dead by the fire and that her mother had taken a big pot of water upstairs to try and revive her.

William recalled his mother going out carrying a large, heavy basket and returning with it empty. He also spoke of going to Wellington with his mother and her asking him to read a bill in the police station to her, about a supposed murder. Finally he told the court that Eliza had treated him and Polly badly, although she had treated seven-year-old Annie well. William and Polly had both been beaten with a lash and Polly had not always been given food at family meals.

At the conclusion of the case, the jury were left to decide whether they believed that Mary Elizabeth Mayo had died naturally or whether she had been unlawfully killed and, if the latter, which of her parents had been guilty of causing her death and if they should be convicted of murder or manslaughter. Given that the medical evidence had been inconsistent with a natural death, they plumped for the latter option, placing the greatest blame for the child's death on Eliza Mayo.

Thus, Eliza was found 'Guilty of manslaughter' and sentenced to twenty years of penal servitude. Thomas Mayo got off lightly. He was only found guilty of being an accessory after the fact and was sentenced to eighteen months imprisonment with hard labour.

15

'YOU HAVE GOT THE WRONG MAN'

Prees Lower Heath, 1887

George Pickerill had spent much of his working life in service to Lord Hill on the Hawkestone estate. Now in his eighties, he had retired to a two-roomed, one-storey cottage on the edge of the estate's timber yard and was in receipt of a small pension from his former employer.

His daughter, Annie Porter, lived nearby at Dogmoor and habitually visited her elderly father to do his shopping and cleaning. On 12 November 1887, Annie visited her father at about nine o'clock in the morning, but found the door of his cottage locked. She went to the old man's bedroom window and knocked, but there was no response. Unable to gain entry, she went to James Adams, a foreman at the timber yard, to ask for his assistance. Having tried unsuccessfully to force the front door, Adams broke a windowpane and opened the window, before climbing through it into the house.

He found George Pickerill lying dead on the floor. His pipe, still filled with un-smoked tobacco, lay beside him. The house was liberally spattered with blood, although none of the furniture in the living area had been disarranged and there was no evidence of a struggle having taken place. George had been savagely beaten about the head and face and his throat had been slashed, presumably with the large, bloodstained butcher's knife which still lay on the kitchen table. He was quite cold and had evidently been dead for some hours.

The police were immediately sent for and PC Barnett of Prees went straight to the cottage and began a search of the premises. He found the key to the locked front door in the garden, approximately 13 yards from the house. Although the living area appeared relatively undisturbed, it was a different story in the cottage bedroom where several items of clothing seemed to have been stolen from the wooden box that George Pickerill had kept under his bed.

By coincidence, his daughter had opened the box only the day before to get some camphor and, although she had not closely examined its contents, she was able to determine that items were missing. Whoever had rifled through George Pickerill's box had not found its secret drawers, one of which still contained three sovereigns and four half-sovereigns. A second secret drawer contained two half crowns and a bankbook.

A search of the garden revealed two pieces of metal, one an iron stanchion and the second described as a 'barrow tang'. Both bore traces of blood, to which a few grey hairs adhered and, when a post-mortem examination, conducted by Dr Venables Williams, determined that the old man had been hit on the back of his head, fracturing his skull, the police surmised that both pieces of metal had probably been used as weapons against him.

The police also found several fresh, if rather indistinct, clog marks in the soft earth outside the cottage, which they measured and documented carefully before covering them with pieces of slate to preserve them from the elements.

It was decided that Mr Pickerill had probably died at around eight o'clock on the evening of 11 November 1887. This was consistent with a statement made by a sawyer, Mr Bradshaw, who had noticed a light in the cottage at around that time.

Enquiries in the neighbourhood revealed that a man named William Arrowsmith had been seen in the vicinity at around the time that George Pickerill's murder was believed to have taken place. Several people had seen Arrowsmith, who was a distant relation of Mr Pickerill's by marriage, carrying what appeared to be bundles of clothes, which he hadn't been carrying the day before. He had even called on one woman, Mrs Barnett, who lived close to Pickerill's cottage, during the early afternoon of 11 November, asking for some matches.

Police began to track William Arrowsmith, finding that, in the days immediately after the murder, he had pawned several items of clothing at pawnshops in Nantwich, Stockport, Hyde and Ashton-under-Lyne. Although Arrowsmith used a series of false names for the transactions, all the garments were subsequently identified as having belonged to George Pickerill.

The police were aware that Arrowsmith had a sister, Mrs Myatt, who lived at Denton, near Manchester and, when they learned that he had left his three children with her, Sergeant Griffiths of Whitchurch went to her home incognito and booked lodgings there. At about seven o'clock on the evening of 17 November, William Arrowsmith walked into the house.

His sister asked him where he had been and he replied that he had been around the Liverpool area, looking for work. Mrs Myatt then told him that her uncle, George Pickerill, had been murdered at Prees Lower Heath.

'You don't say!' responded Arrowsmith, apparently amazed.

Sergeant Griffiths had been listening to this exchange and now asked some questions of his own. He first asked Arrowsmith who he was and then enquired about a cut on his nose, which Arrowsmith said had been the result of a slight accident while he was getting the coal in. Griffiths then introduced himself and arrested Arrowsmith for the murder.

'You have got the wrong man,' Arrowsmith assured him. 'I have not been there the last three weeks and never heard anything about the murder until now.'

In spite of his protests, Arrowsmith was taken into custody and, on being searched at Denton police station, was found to have several pawn tickets in his pockets relating to items that had once belonged to Pickerill. These included a pair of hand-knitted woollen stockings, which had been made for the old man by a neighbour and which Arrowsmith insisted his own wife had knitted for him. There was also a wooden box with coins mounted in the lid, which Arrowsmith swore Pickerill had given to him as a gift three weeks earlier but had been seen in the old man's chest by his daughter on the day before her father's murder. Eventually, Arrowsmith told the police that he had bought the pawn tickets from a tramp.

Griffiths then took possession of Arrowsmith's clogs, which were compared to the footprints outside Pickerill's cottage and found to be a perfect match.

Arrowsmith was charged with the wilful murder of George Pickerill and stood trial at the County Assizes at Shrewsbury, before Mr Justice Smith. Mr Plowden and Mr Jackson prosecuted while Mr Boddam agreed to defend the accused, at the request of the judge.

The prosecution produced what was described in the contemporary newspapers as 'an army of damnatory evidence' against Arrowsmith, leaving their opposing counsel with little opportunity of mustering any credible defence of their client. In the end, the best that the defence counsel could manage was an assertion that Arrowsmith had not been in the area on the day of the murder and that the items that he had subsequently pawned had not been proven to have been present at the property when the old man was killed but could conceivably have been given to him by Pickerill when Arrowsmith last visited him three weeks before his death.

The arguments by the defence counsel proved insufficient to place reasonable doubt in the minds of the jurors, who almost instantly found William Arrowsmith 'Guilty' of the wilful murder of George Pickerill. He was sentenced to death and advised by the judge to hold out no hope whatsoever of a reprieve.

Arrowsmith apparently made a partial confession to prison chaplain, the Revd R.H. Barber, while awaiting his execution. He wrote to his sister in Manchester, asking her to bring his children to visit him and also wrote to another sister who lived near Prees, asking if she could find it in her heart to visit him. Finally, he wrote to George Pickerill's daughter. The letter, dated 22 March 1888, read:

My dear cousin,
I want to write a line to tell you how grievously sorry I am for my great sin, which I confess and to ask you humbly to forgive me. I pray God He may have mercy on my soul for Jesus Christ's sake and that through His merit He may forgive me my terrible sin. [*sic*]

Forty-two-year-old William Arrowsmith was hanged at Shrewsbury Prison by James Berry. In spite of a heavy fall of snow and a bitterly cold north-easterly wind, a crowd of more than 500 people gathered outside the prison to see the black flag hoisted, some even moving to the rear of the prison in order to hear the sound of the drop.

The execution – which was the nineteenth at which Berry had officiated – was remarkable only in that a threatening letter was delivered to the prison, marked for Berry's attention. It appeared to have little to do with the execution of William Arrowsmith but referred to an incident that had occurred many years ago, before Berry even became a hangman. The letter was passed to the police and James Berry did not allow its content to deter him from making a walking tour of Shrewsbury on the morning after the execution. Ever the showman, he was closely followed by a small crowd of people and was later to relate that they 'hung on his every word'.

[Note: In some contemporary accounts of the murder, the victim is alternatively named George Pickering. Pickerill is the most frequently used name, hence I have used it for this account.]

16

'IS HE DEAD THEN?'

Whixall, 1887

William Powell and Elijah Bowes Forrester had once been good friends. Elijah had married Powell's sister in 1885 and, the following year, Powell had bought the farm next door to Elijah's. From that moment on, the relationship between the two men deteriorated, as Powell was now the legal owner of a piece of the lane that ran between his farm and the public road. Forrester was accustomed to using that particular route as a shortcut, something that infuriated Powell, who sought to deny Forrester access.

By November 1887 the bitter feud between Elijah and William had been simmering for some time. Each had accused the other of stealing from him and, in May 1886, Powell filed a complaint against Forrester, accusing him of stealing a dog, a ferret and a tap. The case went before local magistrates and, although it was dismissed due to lack of evidence, it was the final nail in the coffin for any hope of a truce between the two men. Powell became even more determined to prevent Forrester from using his shortcut and erected sheep hurdles to block it. Every time he did so, Forrester simply took them down again.

Then, according to Forrester, Powell took down a gate that belonged to him, one that he had put up to prevent his animals from straying. On 1 November the two men actually squared up to each other on the lane. They didn't physically fight, but traded insults, with Forrester threatening Powell, 'You will get one some night that you will not get up again.'

Powell was not a popular man locally and had managed at one time or another to upset most of his neighbours, to the extent that someone had taken the trouble to compose a rude and slanderous song about him:

There is a man, an Indian red,
Who very seldom sees his bed,
And if it is, it's in the day,
For in the night he cannot stay.

There is a man, an Indian red,
Which all the neighbours do him dread,
The cocks and hens begin to squeak,
When into the hen roost he does sneak.

He married a wife of the Zulu race,
And she is fond of the grovel grace,
She goes to chapel and calls 'Amen',
While he drags the ducks to his den.

One night he went with wit and skill,
And entered into a windymill,
He stole some corn and what? Oh, then
He lugged it right into his den.

He went one day to Ellesmere Fair,
The reins and glasses proved his snare,
The bobbies consulted and hit on a plan,
They went right straight and arrested the man.

When for money he does lack,
Something has to go to rack;
To fulfil his evil desire,
He sets his building all on fire.

The wind blew well, the buildings were dry,
Says he 'My fortune I mean to try'
To rob the insurance was his intent
He struck of a match and away it went.

Some people may take this as a joke,
But in the Narrow Lane he stole the oak,
The bobbies was on his track that night,
But the Red Indian took his flight. [*sic*]

On 17 November 1887, Elijah Forrester chose to march up the road outside Powell's house singing the song very loudly.

Powell, who was sitting indoors with his wife and family, put up with the singing for a few minutes then, when it showed no sign of abating, he went outside to remonstrate with Forrester. Within seconds the singing stopped, but the silence was quickly shattered by the sound of two gunshots in quick succession.

Powell's son, Eli, and his wife, Eliza, immediately ran out of the house and found Powell lying on the ground. By the light of their candles, they could see that he had been shot and, as Eli knelt down to examine his father more closely, he saw Powell's lips move, as if he were trying to speak. However, whatever words he was trying to say were never spoken, as Powell died almost immediately.

The police were summoned and when Constable Bowen arrived, he examined Powell, noticing a gunshot wound in his side. He helped Eli Powell carry his father indoors and then went straight to Forrester's house, where he found a shotgun that had recently been fired.

Bowen then returned to the police station to request back up, returning to Forrester's home with Superintendent Edwards at around midnight. By that time, Forrester had retired to bed, but willingly came down when summoned by the policemen.

'It is a bad thing about Powell', Bowen told Forrester, who immediately responded, 'Is he dead then?' Forrester was arrested and taken to the lock-up at Whitchurch. There he was searched and some gun wadding was found in his pocket. A bag of shot and an unexploded cap were found at his home.

Dr Gwynn from Whitchurch examined the body and found a shotgun wound in Powell's left-hand side. (Curiously, PC Bowen had noted the wound as being on the right-hand side.) At a later post-mortem examination, Gwynn opened Powell's abdominal cavity and found it to be filled with blood, the intestines protruding through the wall of the abdomen. There were no marks of violence anywhere else on the body and none of the blackening of the skin that he would have expected had the gun been in close contact with the deceased when it was fired. Gwynn suggested that the shotgun would have been between 1 and 2 yards away from Powell when the fatal shot was fired and that death would have been almost instantaneous. The doctor retrieved some shotgun pellets from inside Powell's abdomen, which he passed to the police.

An inquest was held at the Waggoner's Inn by coroner Mr G. Warren. The coroner's jury returned a verdict of 'Guilty' of manslaughter against Forrester, but, at the subsequent hearing before magistrates, he was indicted for the wilful murder of William Powell and committed for trial at the next Shropshire Assizes.

The trial opened on 9 March 1888, with Mr Justice Smith presiding over the two charges against Forrester – one of wilful murder, one of manslaughter. Mr Plowden and Mr Lawrence Jackson prosecuted, while Mr Jelf QC and Mr J. Rose appeared for the defence.

The prosecution opened by calling a number of witnesses who testified to hearing Forrester make threats against his brother-in-law and neighbour. At some time, Forrester had allegedly said that he would 'make away with Powell' and that he had bought a gun 'to shoot the Red Indian'. Nobody had taken these threats seriously since Forrester was widely believed to be a non-violent man, and the threats had only been made after he had been drinking. Nevertheless, Forrester had certainly purchased shot for his gun in the week prior to the murder, saying that he intended to use it to shoot pigeons.

Having established both motive and means, the counsel for the prosecution then turned his attention to the night of Powell's death. Mr Plowden first called Thomas Craddock, a farmer who had tried to help Forrester to get a cow over a bridge earlier that evening. Craddock described Forrester as appearing to be sober and in a good mood when he had last seen him heading up the lane towards Powell's farm.

Eliza and Eli Powell were called and both told the court that they had heard the rude song being sung out in the lane shortly before William was shot. Powell's daughter, Rhoda, also heard the singing, as did a near neighbour, Mary Ann Butler. All four people who had heard the song claimed to recognise Elijah Forrester as the singer by his voice, although none of them had actually seen him.

PC Bowen testified about the night of the murder and also about his previous dealings with Powell and Forrester. After one complaint by Powell about his brother-in-law, Bowen had gone to find Forrester and located him outside the Waggoner's Inn, where he had concealed a gun in the hedge. Bowen had reprimanded Forrester for having a gun at night while he was drunk, but Forrester had denied any wrong intentions so Bowen had ordered him to go home, which Forrester had done.

Superintendent Edwards was then called and his evidence corroborated Bowen's. Edwards did, however, state that the shotgun pellets recovered from Powell's body at the post-mortem were of a different size to those found at Forrester's home after his arrest.

Having called Dr Gwynn to the witness box, the prosecution rested and Mr Jelf immediately called two medical witnesses, both of whom contradicted the evidence of Gwynn's post-mortem. Mr John Gill, a member of the Royal College of Surgeons, was an expert in gunshot wounds. He had carried out many experiments using shotguns and believed that blackening of the skin did not occur when the gun was less than 2ft 9in from the body when fired. Thus, it was Gill's contention that Powell could have been holding the barrel of the gun before it went off.

Dr Oliver Pemberton agreed with Gill. He was a senior surgeon at Queen's Hospital, London and also specialised in treating gunshot wounds, having more than forty years experience in that field. He concurred with Gill that a shotgun fired at close range did not always cause blackening of the skin or singeing of the clothes.

Thus the defence counsel maintained that the gun had gone off accidentally in a struggle between Powell and Forrester, probably when Powell had seized the barrel and tried to wrest the weapon away from Forrester.

The defence called one final witness, Robert Woodvine. In the four months between Powell's death and the trial, Woodvine had married Powell's widow. Now Woodvine told the court that he had been out shooting with Elijah Forrester on the day before Powell's death and had offered to make some adjustments to the sight of Forrester's shotgun. He had fully expected Forrester to bring the gun to him for the alteration on 17 November.

When he heard about the shooting shortly after it occurred, Woodvine went to Forrester's father's home where he found Forrester without his gun. The two men had walked home together and during the walk, Woodvine said that Forrester had told him that Powell had grabbed the gun, showing Woodvine a bump on his head that had occurred as a result of the tussle between them. Cross-examined by the prosecution, Woodvine stated that he didn't know why he hadn't reported this conversation to the police and had instead waited until the trial to reveal it for the first time.

With the evidence complete, the jury retired for twenty-five minutes before returning to pronounce Forrester 'Guilty of manslaughter', much to the evident surprise of Mr Justice Smith who appeared to think that 'Guilty of murder' would have been a much more appropriate verdict.

Smith seemed determined that Forrester should be punished as severely as possible and, after consulting with his colleagues, he sentenced Forrester to fifteen years of penal servitude.

17

'WILL NO ONE HELP MY POOR MOTHER?'

Madeley Wood, Ironbridge, 1887

The houses at the top end of Theaves Lane, Madeley Wood, near Ironbridge were some of the poorest dwellings imaginable – basic cottages, with one downstairs room and one upstairs. In 1887, the Bouckley family occupied one of these houses.

The Bouckleys were notorious in the area, particularly the head of the household, George Bouckley, who, although he classed himself as a labourer, had not held a proper job for many years but instead occupied himself with running occasional errands, fetching coal and water to earn his beer money. Any money that he managed to make was invariably spent on himself and he relied on the efforts of his wife and children to maintain the household. Thus, the Bouckleys lived in abject poverty.

George Bouckley was known as a violent and unpredictable man and the fights between him and his wife, Elizabeth, were legendary in the neighbourhood. Bouckley's son had recently left home as a direct result of his father's brutal conduct, the final straw for the young man being when his father allegedly stabbed him. Now Bouckley shared the cottage with his wife and his fifteen-year-old daughter, Annie.

In November 1887, George and his wife were still at odds following an argument that had occurred between them three weeks earlier. Mrs Bouckley had finally had enough of her husband's obnoxious drunken behaviour and the fact that all of his money was spent on alcohol rather than on supporting his family. Following the row, Mrs Bouckley moved out of the marital bed, instead sleeping with her daughter. Yet it appeared that her husband was finally making an effort to control his boorish behaviour and, according to his daughter, had been living a far more temperate life since the quarrel with his wife.

Nevertheless, Mrs Bouckley wasn't quite prepared to share his bed again and, on 11 November, she and Annie retired to bed together at about half past nine, leaving George to sleep alone. Although neither George nor Elizabeth Bouckley had completely put their three-week-old quarrel behind them, they at least seemed to have called a truce. There had been no further arguments between them and they appeared to be on relatively friendly terms. However, George's actions in the early hours of the morning of 12 November were about as far from friendly as it is possible to get.

Annie was abruptly awakened from her sleep by the sound of her mother screaming. Although the room was dark, she could just make out the figure of her father standing by her mother's side of the bed, holding something in his hands. As Annie watched in horror, she saw her father hit her mother twice.

Elizabeth screamed again and, as she did, George turned on his heel and ran downstairs. Annie immediately leaped out of bed and ran after him, just in time to see him taking his razor down from a shelf. Annie didn't wait around to see what he intended to do with it. She ran to the front door, opened it and shouted 'Murder!' at the top of her voice.

Behind her, George Bouckley turned to go back upstairs and Annie bravely tackled him, catching him as he reached the second step.

'I will cut your ******* throat if you interfere,' George growled at her, so Annie let him go, running to the door again and out into the street, yelling 'Murder!' as loudly as she could.

The neighbours were very used to the constant arguments and fights at the Bouckley's house and consequently nobody took the slightest bit of notice of the frantic girl running up and down the street barefoot in her nightdress. The last person who had tried to intervene in a domestic dispute between Mr and Mrs Bouckley had been hit by George with an axe for his pains; hence no one rushed to Annie's assistance. 'Will no one help my poor mother?' Annie begged in desperation, but still nobody came to her aid.

Realising that her efforts to get help were proving fruitless, Annie headed back home, where she found that her mother had managed to get downstairs and was now standing bleeding on the doorstep. Annie then saw her father throw a chopper at Elizabeth, hitting her on her head and knocking her off her feet and into the gutter.

Still, at least she was now out of the house and Annie quickly dragged her to her feet and half carried her down the street. Spotting Mrs Sarah Lamb standing at her window, watching the unfolding drama, Annie begged her, 'Oh, do come down. He has killed my mother.'

Somewhat reluctantly, Sarah Lamb opened her door and Annie pulled her mother inside. At that time, Elizabeth was still conscious and able to talk coherently, telling Mrs Lamb that her husband had done this to her with a coal pick.

Meanwhile, a second neighbour had finally bothered to see what the problem was. Shoemaker Thomas James, who lived about 100 yards away from the Bouckley's house, had been woken from his sleep by screaming and shouting. Well used to the antics of the Bouckley family, James paused for long enough to get dressed and put

A postcard of Ironbridge. (Author's collection)

A postcard of the bridge at Ironbridge. (Author's collection)

The former police station at Ironbridge; it is now a restaurant. (© R. Sly, 2008)

on his hat and coat before walking towards the Bouckley's home, then, thinking he heard someone coming up the street, he dived over a wall and hid, for fear that the passer-by might be George Bouckley. Eventually, he plucked up enough courage to creep closer to the Bouckley's cottage.

The blinds were drawn down in the upstairs window, but James could see that there was a candle burning in the room. As he watched, the flame suddenly went out, whereupon James could hear fearful gurgling and gasping noises coming from within the cottage. He retreated to Mrs Lamb's house, where he broke the news to Annie and Elizabeth that George Bouckley had cut his throat.

At long last the police were called and they in turn sent for a doctor. Sergeant Roberts first went to Mrs Lamb's house and, after being told what had happened, he went down the street to the Bouckley's home. There he found George sprawled on a bed upstairs, wearing only his shirt. A discarded razor lay on the floor, close to the bed, and blood was streaming from a gaping wound in George's throat.

At the time, it was believed that George Bouckley's injuries were more serious than those of his wife, so when surgeon Dr Proctor arrived in Theaves Lane, he only briefly examined Elizabeth before heading for the Bouckley's cottage. Elizabeth was still conscious and lucid and able to tell the doctor that she had woken to find her husband standing over her with a coal pick. He had struck her, but she had eventually managed to get away from him and out into the street.

Dr Proctor found George still alive, although barely, bleeding heavily from a deep slash wound in his throat that had severed his windpipe and all the major blood vessels, penetrating his neck almost through to his spine.

Given the seriousness of Bouckley's wound and his massive blood loss, there was nothing that could be done to help him, and he soon died, after which Dr Proctor turned his attention to Elizabeth. By the time he got back to Mrs Lamb's house, Elizabeth was completely paralysed down one side of her body.

An inquest into the death of George Bouckley was convened at the Golden Ball Inn, close to the Bouckley's home, before Dr Taylor, the coroner for the borough of Wenlock. However, just after the jury had been sworn in and had gone to view George's body, the news reached the coroner that Elizabeth had succumbed to her injuries, Dr Taylor decided to hold both inquests together and the jury was re-sworn. The coroner then revealed that George and Elizabeth had never been legally married and thus nobody was sure of Elizabeth's real name. At various times, she had been known as Elizabeth Bartlam, Elizabeth Wilkinson and Elizabeth Wellings, so the coroner stated that he proposed to continue with the proceedings as if Elizabeth's name had been Bouckley.

The inquest jury first heard from Annie Bouckley, then from Dr Proctor. He testified that George Bouckley had died as a result of massive haemorrhage, having cut his own throat. Proctor told the inquest that George had three other small cuts on his throat as well as the major wound that had eventually killed him and that George's razor had been so blunt that it was a miracle that it had managed to inflict any injury at all. 'He must have had a most determined hold of it,' said the doctor. Proctor was the Bouckley's regular doctor and told the coroner that George could not have been said to be in his right mind for some time.

The next witness to be called was Thomas James, who related his account of hearing the commotion and of pausing to get dressed and put on his hat and coat before going out to investigate. 'You take a deal of care of yourself,' the coroner told him rather sarcastically. James explained that he knew the Bouckley's 'games' and had been there before. (It had been James who had tried to intervene in a previous argument between the Bouckley's and been hit with an axe.) James admitted to being afraid of George Bouckley.

After hearing from Sergeant Roberts, the jury returned a verdict of *felo de se* – meaning 'self murder' – on George Bouckley. They then turned their attention to the death of his 'wife', Elizabeth.

Although the two inquests were held consecutively, they were each separate legal proceedings, which meant that Annie was recalled to repeat her evidence. It must have been a terrible ordeal for the young girl who, it must be remembered, had just lost her father and had heard only a short while before that her mother had now died too.

Sarah Lamb testified and Dr Proctor was then asked to give his assessment of Elizabeth's injuries, which he described as four head wounds and a broken arm. One of the wounds on the back of her head was three inches in diameter, while another had penetrated her skull so that her brain matter protruded through the wound. Proctor described the depth of the wound by telling the inquest that he had been able to insert his finger directly into Elizabeth's brain. It was this wound that had ultimately been the cause of her death.

Three weapons were then shown to the jury – a small pick, sharpened at each end, a chopper and a hammer, all of which were bloodstained. It was Proctor's opinion that the pick had caused the penetrating wound, while the larger wound to the back of the head had been caused when the chopper had been thrown at Mrs Bouckley as she left the house.

The coroner's jury returned a verdict of wilful murder against Bouckley and the case was closed. It can only be assumed that George Bouckley was insane at the time of the murder, since there appears to have been no real motive for the killing. In the past, in the heat of arguments, he had often threatened his wife that he would kill her some day, but, when he finally carried out his threat, he did so at a time when their relationship was considerably less stormy than it usually was. There had been nothing to precipitate the killing of Elizabeth Bouckley and her husband's subsequent suicide.

The local newspaper of the time reports that, in the days immediately following the murder, people flocked to the scene, drawn by a morbid curiosity to view the squalid little cottage where the tragedy occurred. The ultimate fate of poor Annie Bouckley is not recorded.

[Note: The contemporary newspaper accounts of the case show several different variations of the spelling of the name Bouckley, including Boucley and Buckley.]

18

'I HAVE KILLED THE BEST LITTLE WOMAN ON EARTH'

Much Wenlock, 1898

William Lawley had a great many business and personal interests in and around the town of Much Wenlock. He had recently owned one of the local gas works, until it was acquired by the town council, and he was also a collector of rates, a registrar of births, marriages and deaths, the secretary of the local Friendly Society, an active member of the Wenlock Olympian Society and the church choir, as well as the organiser of the local race meeting.

Prior to selling the gas works, Lawley was apparently a bright, cheerful character and an astute businessman. However, having disposed of his business he became dejected, morose and irritable, and soon it appeared that his mind had become completely unhinged. He was convinced that people were stealing from him and also believed that he did not have long to live and was terrified by the idea that his wife might survive him and marry someone else. Finally, he feared that he was transmitting some kind of evil influence to his children. Early in 1897, he was sent to Southport for a rest cure. He returned much improved, but it was only a temporary respite, and his mental illness soon returned. After making an attempt to strangle his wife, Helen, and attacking George Langford, one of his employees, he was certified insane and admitted as a private patient to Coton Hill Asylum in Stafford in August 1897, leaving Helen to cope with his various business commitments as best she could.

After his mental health had improved sufficiently for him to be discharged from the asylum for a trial period, Lawley went to lodge with his sister in Manchester where he lived until 16 July 1898, when he impulsively decided to pay a surprise visit to his home at Much Wenlock. Having caught the overnight mail train from Manchester to Shrewsbury, he went to the yard of cab proprietor Mr Franklin on Swan Hill and hired a cab, giving his name as William Jones. He rode as far as Harley Bank, about 2 miles from Much Wenlock, alighting from the cab at half-past four in the morning, then walked the rest of the way home.

At around seven o'clock on the morning of 17 July, Mrs Lawley and her fourteen-year-old daughter Violet May were still asleep. Roused from her bed by loud knocking on the door, Helen walked downstairs in her nightdress to see who was there and was startled to see her husband standing on the doorstep. As Mrs Lawley turned back to go to her bedroom to get dressed, her husband followed her and, four or five steps up the stairs, he drew a new razor from his pocket and, grabbing his wife from behind, he cut her throat from ear to ear.

On hearing the commotion, Violet bravely rushed out of the bedroom, seeing her mother and father grappling together near the bottom of the stairs. Her mother told her to open the window and shout for help, but realising that there were likely to be very few people up and about so early on a Sunday morning, Violet instead seized the heavy piece of oak that was used to secure the back door. The girl struck out at her father with the post, hitting him twice on the head, after which he immediately fled the house.

Much Wenlock. (© N. Sly, 2008)

As soon as he had left, Violet and her mother ran out of the back door and into the street, where Helen was overcome with faintness. With difficulty, Violet half dragged, half carried her mother to the home of Mr Francis Danks, a schoolmaster who lived opposite. Danks was awakened by someone hammering frantically on his front door and a woman's voice calling, 'Oh, do open the door.' Danks immediately ran downstairs, finding Violet and her mother on his doorstep in their nightdresses and bare feet, both covered with blood.

'Oh, Mr Danks, do take us in. My father has done this,' Violet sobbed. Danks helped the two women into his home where Helen Lawley promptly collapsed onto the hall floor, blood streaming from her ravaged throat. Violet also sank to the floor, lifting her mother's head onto her lap and holding her hand.

Danks knelt to attempt first aid, but a closer examination of Helen's wound suggested that any such efforts would be futile. He rushed upstairs to throw on a few clothes, then, partially dressed, ran to summon assistance. As he hurried to fetch the local police constable, PC Evans, Danks met William Lawley on the street. The two men passed without speaking.

Although Danks was only absent for a couple of minutes, on his return it was obvious that Helen Lawley was close to death and, at five minutes past seven o'clock, she died in her daughter's arms, having first indicated that Violet should kiss her cheek. Just minutes later, Dr Hart and Dr Mackenzie arrived; sadly they were too late to do any more than pronounce life extinct.

Dr Mackenzie had been the Lawley's family physician for sixteen years and had attended William Lawley throughout his mental illness. Now, assisted by Dr Hart, he conducted a post-mortem examination on the body of Helen Lawley, finding a 4in-long transverse cut across her throat, which had completely severed her windpipe and partially severed her jugular vein, leading to her death from loss of blood. There were also several cuts on her hands and fingers, apparently caused when she had tried unsuccessfully to grab the razor from her husband.

Having been alerted of the tragedy by Mr Danks, PC Evans immediately went in search of William Lawley who had returned to his home and was standing at the kitchen door. Moments earlier, he had calmly greeted postman Harry Troth as he delivered a parcel to the house, but now his calmness had completely deserted him and he vigorously resisted Evans's attempts to arrest him, pleading to be allowed to go inside the house, just for a minute. With the aid of Mr James Bizzell and Mr John Elcock, Evans finally subdued Lawley and he was taken into custody. When searched on arrival at the police station, a razor, a bloodstained handkerchief, two pawn tickets in the name of William Jones, a railway ticket, some small change and a locket were found in his pockets. He had apparently pawned his watch and chain to raise the money to buy a new razor and pay his rail fare from Manchester.

Lawley was brought before magistrates the following morning, charged with the murder of his wife. By now he was calm and rational again, explaining to the court that he had not been accountable for his actions for the past year. His sister in Manchester had supplied him with alcohol, believing that it would do him good

The court room at the Guildhall, Much Wenlock. (Author's collection)

and this had maddened him and caused him to kill his wife. Telling the court, 'I have killed the best little woman on earth', he expressed regret for his actions, saying that he should never have been allowed to leave the asylum in Stafford.

Violet Lawley, who was staying with friends at the Stork Hotel, was by now in a state of near collapse due to shock. Her older brother, Frank, was summoned back to Much Wenlock by telegram, but learned of his mother's tragic death by reading a newspaper report on his journey home.

Helen Lawley's funeral was held at the parish church, just across the street from her home. Afterwards, Violet was taken to live with her aunt and uncle, Thomas and Ann Woof, at their home in Kingswinford near Stourbridge.

William Lawley was committed for trial for the wilful murder of his wife and the proceedings opened at Shrewsbury before Mr Justice Ridley on 30 November 1898. Mr Rowlett and Mr Astley conducted the prosecution and Mr A. Graham and Mr Harold Hardy were retained as defence counsel. However, without even hearing the case for the defence, the jury returned a verdict of 'Guilty, but insane', leaving Mr Justice Ridley to order Lawley to be detained as a criminal lunatic until her Majesty's pleasure be known.

19

'NO DOUBT HE IS THE ROOT OF ALL THE EVIL'

Broseley, 1900

On the afternoon of 27 January 1900, Francis Henry Martin, a solicitor's clerk for the firm Potts & Potts in Broseley, was walking towards Willey when he spotted a woman sitting on the ground, leaning against a fir tree, a bundle at her feet. When he went for a closer look, he realised that the woman was dead and that the bundle was in fact the body of a little girl.

Martin ran for a policeman. The woman was soon identified as Harriett Meyrick Edwards, aged twenty-two, and the child as her four-year-old daughter, Charlsie Margaret Edwards. Both bodies were fully clothed and there was no sign of any struggle having taken place at the scene of their deaths. An empty glass jar was found next to Miss Edwards.

A post-mortem examination, carried out on the following morning by Dr Boon of Broseley, found that the woman had severe chemical burns to her face and neck. Her hands were tightly clenched into fists and her tongue, lips and the roof of her mouth were badly blistered. Charlsie's little body was similarly affected and she also had severe chemical burns to her left hand. Before death she had been a normal, healthy child, who had obviously been well cared for and well nourished. The doctor determined that both Harriett and Charlsie had died from drinking carbolic acid, pointing out that it was an excruciatingly painful means of dying.

An inquest was held at Dean Corner Farm, Willey, by Mr F.H. Potts, the borough coroner. First to speak at the inquest was servant George Edwards, who stated that the deceased woman was his sister, the child his niece.

93

Broseley. (© N. Sly, 2008)

Charlsie was illegitimate and Harriett had always been tight-lipped about the identity of the child's father, although he was assumed to be Harry Adams, Harriett's long-term boyfriend, who paid 2s each week as maintenance for the little girl. George had last seen his sister on the evening of 23 January, when she had appeared 'a little low'. Harriett had made no complaint to her brother, however, and he had no idea why she should be depressed or want to commit suicide – he had never heard her threaten to do so.

Harriett's landlady, Ann Lloyd, of Foundry Lane, Broseley, was next to address the inquest. Harriett and her daughter had lodged with her for four months, and she had last seen them on the evening of 24 January when the couple had come downstairs on their way out of the house. Harriett had not spoken, but Charlsie had told the landlady, 'You've not got a nice little dress like me.'

According to Mrs Lloyd, Harriett had not been to work that day and she seemed especially 'low-spirited'. Two days earlier, Harry Adams had whistled outside the house and Harriet had gone out to see him. Adams had told her that he was intending to go to a dancing class at The Cape. As far as Mrs Lloyd knew, Adams had always been regular with his maintenance payments for Charlsie, although Harriett had complained to her in the past that he was bad.

After Harriett's death, Mrs Lloyd found two letters in her room, one under her pillow and one on a box next to her bed. These were now read out to the inquest, the first being a suicide note, the second a letter dealing with the disposal of Harriett's worldly goods after her death.

The first letter read:

> Dear father and aunt, when you get this I shall be dead, I am tired of life, and have been. I am sorry to cause you so much bother, but see to me being buried respectfully. I don't want Aunt Hannah nor Rogers to follow me. I should like to be buried at Barrow, but wherever Harry is buried put me with him and little Cissy. We shall take her, too – she will have no one to look after her when we have gone. Me and Harry have resolved to die together. Nothing to live for here. I can't write any more. Tell poor old dad not to worry. I must close, and good-bye from Harriett. [*sic*]

The letters were just two of many found in Harriett's room after her death. The police had read them all, but had found nothing in their contents to implicate anybody in the deaths of Harriett and her daughter.

Mrs Lloyd finished her evidence by stating that Harriett had been a good mother to Charlsie and had always appeared very fond of the child. Mrs Lloyd had never heard Harriett threaten suicide although, according to Mrs Lloyd, she constantly seemed depressed and never laughed. Before finally stepping down, Mrs Lloyd identified the glass jar found with the bodies as one that belonged to Harriett, who had bought it filled with marmalade.

The inquest then heard from a woman named Eliza Leadbetter, who had known Harriett well. Eliza testified that recently Harriett had been somewhat obsessed by a local body of water known as the Marsh Pool. Harriett had tried to persuade Eliza to go there with her, saying that she wanted to know its depth. Eliza had refused to go and Harriett had said that she would go by herself one day.

Eliza had last seen Harriett on the Tuesday before her death. Both women worked at Benthall's Pottery and, during their lunch break, Harriett had asked her if she had been to the dance at The Cape on the previous day. When Eliza said that she had, Harriett began to question her about Harry Adams. Was he there? Eliza replied that he was. Had he been with the Ball girls? Eliza said that he hadn't seemed to be with anyone in particular. Harriett seemed much relieved by this answer, telling Eliza that she had heard that Harry was walking out with one of the two sisters named Ball. Eliza concluded her statement by telling the inquest that, in her final days, Harriett 'appeared to have something on her mind'. She had not been to work on the following day.

Chemist George Egglestone was next to speak, saying that, in the week before her death, Harriett had come to his shop one evening and asked to purchase some laudanum. Egglestone had refused to sell her any since she did not have a prescription from a doctor and, on asking her why she wanted it, he was told that Harriett was having difficulty sleeping. The chemist had offered to make her a sleeping draught and she had accepted, paying 1s for the mixture. According to Egglestone, Harriett had not tried to purchase any carbolic acid and indeed, despite their thorough investigations, the police had never managed to find out from where she had obtained the chemical.

Having heard all the evidence, the coroner told the jury that it appeared as though Harriett were very much in love with Harry Adams and that it seemed as though that love had not been reciprocated in the way she would have wanted. Potts told the court that a subpoena had been drawn up for Harry Adams to attend the inquest, but he had left the area and the police had been unable to find him to serve the order on him. Having heard all the evidence, the coroner couldn't see that Adams' attendance would have made much difference, but, nevertheless, Adams should have acted like a man and attended the proceedings.

'No doubt he is the root of all the evil,' interjected the foreman of the coroner's jury, Mr Edmund Hodgkinson.

Surprisingly, nothing whatsoever was said about the contents of Harriett's suicide note, which seemed to indicate that she believed that she and Adams had made a suicide pact, agreeing to take Charlsie with them. The coroner continued to say that it seemed as though Harriett's mind had become unhinged over a period of time before her death and the jury agreed, finding that Charlsie was wilfully murdered by her mother, who afterwards committed suicide whilst temporarily insane.

20

'I LOVED HER AND NOBODY ELSE SHALL HAVE HER'

Westbury, 1901

Richard Wigley had once been a successful and prosperous butcher, holding a profitable stall on Shrewsbury market. However, his marriage had failed, after which he had increasingly turned to drink. By November 1901, Wigley was in arrears with his maintenance payments and was taken to court by his estranged wife, to whom he then owed more than £4. Wigley told the court that he had no money, having been out of work, but it later emerged that he had in fact borrowed sufficient money to pay off his debts in full, which he intended to do only if there was a danger that he would be sent to prison for non-payment. When this didn't happen, Wigley left the court, having promised to settle all his debts within one month, when he found work. With money in his pockets, he began drinking and didn't stop.

On 30 November, Wigley rose early and put on his butcher's apron, with a knife-sharpening steel attached to a strap worn around his waist and his large butcher's knife in a leather pouch. When Wigley went downstairs at his lodgings at Hill's Lane, Shrewsbury, another lodger, Joseph Malloy, was already up and was busy lighting a fire. Having carefully sharpened his knife, Wigley shook hands with Malloy and wished him 'Goodbye', adding that he probably wouldn't see him again. He then set out to walk to Westbury. On his way, he sold his apron, steel and knife to his cousin Edward Nicholls, a butcher at Bowbridge and, with the proceeds he bought several pints of beer.

Eliza Mary Bowen was twenty-eight years old and worked as a barmaid at the Lion Inn at Westbury. She had left her job there two years previously to work for

Charles Allen at Berrington. It was at Berrington that she had apparently first met Richard Wigley, who had been employed as a slaughter man in the village. Bowen and Wigley first became close friends and then lovers and for some time, Wigley tried unsuccessfully to persuade Eliza to become his housekeeper. Her persistent refusal seemed to irritate Wigley and several times he threatened that, if she would not be his housekeeper then he would ensure that she would never be housekeeper to anyone else.

Eventually, Eliza seemed to tire of the relationship. She left her job in Berrington and, on 12 August 1901, returned to her previous employment at the Lion Inn, where her sister, Kate, worked as the manageress. Wigley tried to visit Eliza at the pub, but she seemed somewhat ambivalent towards him. Having told her sister that Wigley was in the habit of insulting her, in September, Eliza wrote Wigley a letter:

My Dear Dick, I daresay you are surprised have not heard from me, not seen me but will write you again. I will be in town one of these first days hoping you are well. I am better. Have not been well at all this last week. I have no news to tell you because it is very quiet here. Hoping to see you this next week. I close with love to you. I remain truly, E. BOWEN. Be sure and don't come here again. [*sic*]

At just before ten o'clock on the morning of Saturday 30 November, servant Ellen Richards saw Richard Wigley approaching the Lion Inn as she was breakfasting in the kitchen with Eliza Bowen. Wigley had apparently been something of a

The Lion Inn, Westbury. (© N. Sly, 2008)

nuisance to the barmaid, turning up unexpectedly and following her around as she went about her work. Ellen alerted Eliza to Wigley's arrival and Eliza went into the bar, where she served him with two or three glasses of beer. Wigley then asked Eliza for another drink 'on trust', to which Eliza responded that she didn't trust any man.

At this point, much to her annoyance, Wigley grabbed hold of Eliza, who ordered him to 'Loose me, man,' and, turning to Ellen Richards, asked her to go for a policeman. At this, Wigley let go of Eliza but continued to follow her around, all the while trying to talk to her and being repulsed.

Shortly afterwards, Eliza went to the wine cupboard, which was located in a passageway close to the front door of the pub. Once again, Wigley was at her heels like a faithful puppy and, as she reached the hallway, he grabbed her again. Eliza asked Ellen Richards to take the quart jug that she was holding and, as Ellen moved forward to do so, she noticed Wigley, who by then had his left arm around Eliza's throat, drawing a knife from his pocket.

Ellen didn't wait around to see what happened next, but fled screaming from the pub to the home of blacksmith Robert Rogers, who lived about 60 yards away. Rogers immediately went back to the pub with Ellen but, by the time they got there, Eliza Bowen was staggering around outside the front door, blood gushing from a wound in her throat. As Rogers approached her, Eliza suddenly turned and tottered back into the pub, eventually collapsing in the hall, her head almost severed from her body.

By now, Ellen's frantic screams had drawn a number of men to the pub and, emerging calmly from a side door, Wigley announced to them that he had killed Miss Bowen for love. He made no effort to escape, instead waiting quietly for a policeman to arrive and arrest him. When PC George Teece, the Westbury village policeman, arrived on the scene, Wigley told him, 'I have killed that little woman. It's all for love. I loved her and nobody else shall have her.' Teece handcuffed Wigley and searched him, finding a bloody clasp-knife in his right-hand trouser pocket. Charged with the wilful murder of Eliza Bowen, Richard Wigley seemed quite philosophical, saying to Superintendent Eli Elcock, 'I killed her and shall swing for it'.

Wigley told the arresting officers that he had left a letter in the bar. It was Eliza's letter, in which she had instructed him, 'Be sure and don't come here again.' On the back of it, he had scribbled a note in pencil to Eliza's sister, Kate: 'Dear Kate, I have killed your sister. I loved her and will die for her.'

Dr Howie, a surgeon from Westbury, had immediately been summoned, arriving to find Eliza Bowen lying on her back in the hall, her dress drawn up to her knees. She had a large wound across her throat, severing her windpipe and arteries, which had bled so copiously that Eliza had lost almost all the blood from her body. Expressing surprise that Eliza had managed to stagger out into the road and then return to the pub after being injured, Howie gave his opinion that her death was due to blood loss and would have occurred within one minute of the wound being inflicted.

An inquest was convened into the death of Eliza Bowen, at which the jury recorded a verdict of wilful murder against Richard Wigley. Wigley was by then in custody at Shrewsbury Gaol and, although he was given the opportunity of attending the inquest, he refused to do so.

His trial opened before Mr Justice Phillimore on 27 February 1902. Mr R.H. Amphlett KC presented the case for the prosecution, assisted by Mr L.R. Wilkinson. Almost up until the commencement of the proceedings, Richard Wigley had refused to appoint any defence counsel – as far as he was concerned, he had committed the crime and just wanted to die. However, just before the trial opened, Wigley unexpectedly accepted an offer for a lawyer to be appointed to act on his behalf and, on the day before, Mr S.R.G. Bosanquet was given the thankless task of hurriedly building a case for the defence.

When asked by the judge if he pleaded 'Guilty' or 'Not Guilty', Wigley replied, 'I don't know. I did not know what I was doing that morning.' The judge interpreted this as a plea of 'Not Guilty'.

When Wigley had appeared before magistrates, charged with Eliza Bowen's murder, the court had been given the impression that he and the deceased were just good friends. Now it emerged that their relationship had been a much more intimate one and that, and while Eliza Bowen had been working at Berrington she would regularly pretend to go to bed then sneak downstairs and let Wigley into the house. Wigley had also arranged lodgings for Eliza Bowen in Shrewsbury, at which he had been a regular visitor. When she had moved back to Westbury, Wigley had become concerned about Eliza's relationship with the pub landlord, William Vaughan, a prosperous farmer who also owned other inns in the area. Vaughan stated in court that he had not been aware of any doubts that Wigley might have entertained about the propriety of his relationship with his employee, agreeing with the defence counsel that any such allegations against him were delusions on Wigley's part.

It was left to the counsel for the defence to try and argue what was effectively an open and shut case against his client. Mr Bosanquet had discovered that Wigley's mother had spent some time as an in-patient at a lunatic asylum while Wigley was a boy and Bosanquet maintained that his client had inherited this insanity and that it had lain dormant in him until awakened by love and jealousy.

Bosanquet pointed out to the jury that several prosecution witnesses had given evidence that supported this claim. Mrs Elizabeth Taylor, Wigley's landlady at the time of the murder, had testified that Wigley had once told her that Eliza Bowen was his only friend in the world. Wigley, said Taylor, had led a very unhappy life and was often morose and gloomy. Yet, when he was drunk – as he often was – he behaved like a madman. Wigley's employer, for whom he had worked for almost two years, said almost the same thing – while sober, Wigley was quiet, yet in drink he became excited and very noisy.

The defence counsel went on to tell the jury that Wigley was insane at the time of the murder and also very drunk, having consumed several pints of beer on an empty stomach. As further evidence, he asked the jury to consider the note that Wigley

Mr Justice Phillimore.
(Author's collection)

had hastily scribbled on the back of Eliza's letter. According to Bosanquet, rightly or wrongly, Wigley's jealousy had been aroused. From that moment 'his madness instantly sprang into life and, from that day, as far as Miss Bowen was concerned, he was possessed of a fixed, insane idea, ever impelling him on to the final catastrophe.'

Mr Justice Phillimore summed up the case for the jury, telling them that there was no doubt that Eliza Bowen had not wished Wigley to visit her at the Lion Inn, probably through fear that her character would be blackened if it was known that she was receiving visits from a married man. He then went on to clarify the matter of insanity, saying that thinking that he could take the law into his own hands was not a sign of insanity in a man – rather that man was either foolish, or criminal, or both. Insanity must be a strong delusion, sufficiently so to remove all of a man's judgement, rather than a mere passion. For insanity to be proven, a man should be rendered so incapable by disease of the mind as to be completely unaware of the nature of the act he committed. Neither was drinking to excess an excuse, said the judge. The only occasion on which it could be considered more than a contributory factor was when it made a man mad, rather than, as in this case, simply made a man passionate and unreasonable because drink was upon him. Wigley was known to have been quick-tempered and passionate and, although there was evidence of a hereditary taint of insanity, it was for the defence to prove to the jury beyond any reasonable doubt that he was insane at the time of the murder.

The jury retired for eight minutes, returning to pronounce Richard Wigley 'Guilty' of the wilful murder of Eliza Mary Bowen. The judge turned to Wigley and asked if he had anything to say before sentence was passed upon him.

Wigley immediately told the court that Mr Vaughan's evidence had been untrue. He maintained that he had rarely visited Eliza Bowen at the Lion Inn that summer, and he then sensationally stated that Eliza in fact had three children, all fathered by her employer. Wigley also complained that he had not had a chance to address any of the witnesses or to ask questions or contradict their false testimony.

Wigley's assertions had no effect on the judge, who pronounced the death sentence, which Wigley accepted calmly and without protest. However, a large crowd of spectators had attended the court and, at the close of the proceedings, Vaughan found himself being heckled by a number of hostile people, mainly youths and children, who followed him *en masse* to Shrewsbury railway station, where police prevented them from pursuing Vaughan onto the platform.

Awaiting his execution at Shrewsbury Gaol, Wigley appeared resigned to his fate. He told Mr Fletcher, the prison chaplain:

> If the prison gates were thrown open and I was told I could have a free pardon if I told how I did it, I could not do so. It was done, but I don't know how I did it. The only thing I remember was wiping the knife after I had done the deed and I don't remember why I did it.

In his last days, several people visited Wigley, including Edward Frances, a young man who had been adopted in infancy by Wigley and his estranged wife. Wigley's wife also visited him and the couple reconciled their differences.

Henry Pierrepoint carried out Wigley's execution on 18 March 1902, assisted by John Ellis. Fifty-four-year-old Wigley went to the gallows almost willingly, having accepted full responsibility for the murder, for which he expressed a deep and sincere penitence. He had spoken at length about the murder to the prison chaplain who, after the execution, spoke out about the effects of drink, pointing out that Wigley had consumed 2s 4d worth of beer on an empty stomach before committing the murder. Wigley, said the chaplain, had never intended to kill Eliza Bowen and had no recollection of actually doing so. 'Drink has been my curse and ruin,' Wigley had told the chaplain, saying that, if he had his time over again, he would never touch alcohol.

[Note: There are various discrepancies in contemporary newspaper accounts of the murder and subsequent trial, particularly regarding Richard Wigley's age, which, at the time of his execution, is variously given as both thirty-four and fifty-four years old. As Wigley is described as 'an elderly man' and 'past middle-age' and Eliza was said to be a 'comparatively young woman', the latter estimate seems more probable. The names of some witnesses also vary – blacksmith Robert Rogers is also referred to as Herbert Rogers.]

21

'DON'T, FOR THE SAKE OF THE CHILDREN'

For thirteen-year-old Henry Cox, home life in Upper Galdeford, Ludlow, was akin to living in a war zone, as his parents, Thomas and Elizabeth, fought and bickered every day, from morning until night. Henry was forced to grow up before his time, trying in vain to keep the peace between them and to shield his younger brother, Benjamin, from the worst of their anger.

His parents' behaviour had been no different from normal on 10 August 1917 and, when Henry went to bed, they were still arguing, with Thomas accusing Elizabeth of spreading lies about him around the town. The whole family slept in the same bedroom and in the early hours of the morning, Henry woke to a continuation of the earlier argument as his father angrily demanded of Elizabeth, 'What do you want to tell so many lies about me for?'

Henry didn't hear his mother's response, but moments later she screamed loudly as her husband lashed out at her before he abruptly left the room. Henry lit a lamp and his mother asked him if he would go and get some water for her, so that she could bathe her head. While the boy was fetching a basin of water, he heard his mother screaming again, this time far more desperately than before.

He raced upstairs to find his mother lying on the bedroom floor, pleading with her husband, 'Don't, for the sake of the children'.

'Has he cut your throat?' Henry asked her and, when Elizabeth said 'Yes' he turned to his father and asked him why he had done that.

'She should not tell so many lies about me. She is canting all over the town about me', was Thomas's explanation. Henry realised that his father had not only slit his mother's throat but had also slashed his own. He asked Thomas if he should run and fetch his aunt.

Upper Galdeford, Ludlow. (© N. Sly, 2008)

'If you don't shut up and go into bed, I'll hit you under the ear,' was Thomas Cox's reply, and the frightened boy immediately did as he was told.

Somehow, Henry managed to fall asleep again until his father woke him at half-past seven in the morning and told him to go to a neighbour's house and raise the alarm. Henry actually ran to the familiarity of his aunt's house in Old Street where he roused his aunt, Mary Ward, from her bed by knocking frantically at her door. Mary called the police and PC Charles Morris accompanied her and Henry back to the Cox's home. There they found Elizabeth Cox lying on the bedroom floor, dead due to a massive haemorrhage from a cut across her throat. Thomas was sitting up in bed, his own throat slashed from ear to ear, weak from loss of blood. When questioned by the police officer, all he could say was, 'I don't know what made me do it. It's a bad job. I ought not to have done it.'

Cox was taken to hospital where surgeons managed to patch him up sufficiently to stand trial at the Shropshire Assizes on 8 November for the wilful murder of his wife. The trial was presided over by Mr Justice Atkin, with D. Cotes-Preedy prosecuting and Alexander Graham defending.

It emerged at the trial that Cox was usually bearded and never shaved, thus having no personal use for a razor. In his own defence, Cox told the court that, on the day before the death of his wife, he had heard that his eldest son, Thomas, a soldier, was coming home on leave from France. He had bought the razor as a gift for his son. The prosecution, however, argued that the razor had been bought with a different purpose in mind and that purpose was to kill Elizabeth Cox.

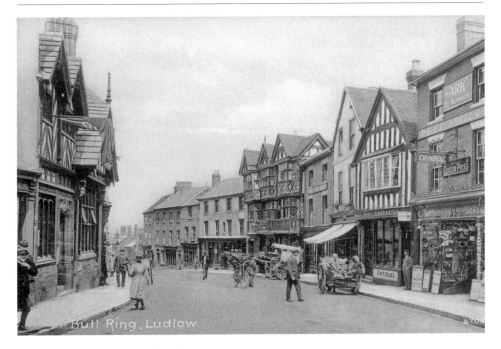

A postcard of Ludlow. (Author's collection)

Ludlow High Street. (Author's collection)

Ludlow Magistrate's Court. (© N. Sly, 2008)

Cox, who earned his living as a hawker, denied that he had mistreated his wife in the past and that there had been occasions when the police had been called to deal with allegations of his domestic violence against her. He insisted that he could recall very little of the night of his wife's murder and that the first thing he remembered was someone coming into his bedroom in the morning and shouting at him to 'Get up! Get up!'

For the defence, Alexander Graham tried to convince the jury that his client had been insane at the time of the murder, stating that Cox had attempted to commit suicide once before. However, the jury were unable to accept this argument, finding sixty-year-old Thomas Cox 'Guilty of the wilful murder of his wife' and leaving the judge with just one option – to sentence Cox to death.

The defence immediately applied for leave to appeal the sentence on the grounds that they wished to call further evidence of Cox's insanity at the time of the murder, particularly in respect of his previous suicide attempt. The Court of Criminal Appeal, under Mr Justice Darling, ruled that, when a full trial had taken place and questions had arisen into the sanity of the defendant, the Home Secretary was better placed to investigate the matter than the courts. Hence Cox's appeal was dismissed and, as the Home Secretary saw no reason to intervene, Thomas Cox was hanged at Shrewsbury Prison on 19 December 1917. John Ellis carried out the execution, assisted by William Wills.

22

'I DON'T REMEMBER DOING IT'

Church Stretton, 1924

Friday 24 October 1924 in Church Stretton was unusual only in that the grocer's shop run by John Doughty in Sandford Avenue was not open for business as it normally was. The shop was situated close to a busy café and, at just after nine o'clock in the morning, a child playing in the café's back garden reported hearing a strange moaning sound coming from the rear of Doughty's shop.

When errand boy Harry Davies arrived for work, he found the shop still locked up. When there was no response to his knocks on the door, he went round to the rear of the property, where he found his employer lying unconscious in the yard. His calls for help were heard by Harold Holmes, who ran through the café and scrambled over a 6ft-high brick wall to gain access into Doughty's yard. It took a moment or two for Holmes to notice the open window, 23ft above the yard, and he instantly assumed that John Doughty had somehow fallen through it. Finding it strange that there was no trace of Doughty's wife, Edith, and their three-year-old daughter, Kathleen, he began to hammer on the back door.

By now a crowd of people had gathered at the rear of the café and were peering curiously over the wall, so Holmes sent someone to fetch the police and a doctor, while he began to systematically try all the doors and windows at the rear of the premises, spurred on to greater efforts when he thought he heard a faint groaning coming from inside the house. Finally, he found an insecure window, which he climbed through, to be met by an unbelievable scene of carnage.

Edith Doughty and young Kathleen had been savagely attacked in the kitchen, which was saturated with their blood. Edith lay on her left side by the fireplace while her daughter lay on her back a short distance away. Both had serious head

Sandford Avenue, Church Stretton, 1950s. (Author's collection)

Sandford Avenue as it is today. (© N. Sly, 2008)

wounds but were still alive. Edith was unconscious, while Kathleen was making the occasional convulsive movement. Holmes realised that he could do nothing to help them, so left the house to check that the police and a doctor had been called.

When Dr Higginson arrived just minutes later, he found both mother and daughter to be so severely injured that he held out little hope for their recovery. Nevertheless, both were rushed to Salop Royal Infirmary, where Kathleen died at midday and Edith at ten o'clock that evening.

Having attended to Edith and Kathleen, Dr Higginson turned his attention to John, eventually driving him in his car to the Church Stretton Infirmary, where Doughty soon regained consciousness. He was found to have no broken bones, but to be suffering the effects of concussion and to have a back injury. It was noted that his clothes were bloodstained and, having found no evidence of any intruder at the shop, the police concluded that Doughty must have been in the immediate vicinity when his wife and daughter were slaughtered. Other than the presence of the two nearly dead bodies, there was no sign of any disturbance or of any forced entry at the shop and nothing appeared to have been stolen. A large axe, obviously the murder weapon, was propped up against a chair in the kitchen and all the doors and windows had been secured from the inside. The only exception was the small window through which Harold Holmes had gained entry into the property and that was extremely stiff to open and close. It was doubtful that anyone who had left the house through that window would have taken the extra time and effort needed to shut it behind him or herself.

Doughty was transferred under police guard to the Royal Salop Infirmary and, on 25 October 1924, he was formally charged with the murder of his family, which he immediately denied. In addition to his physical injuries, Doughty was extremely psychologically damaged, sufficiently so for him to be certified insane.

Known as an extremely private man, John Doughty had been married to Edith for only five years. It was his second marriage. His first wife had suffered from rheumatoid arthritis and so severe was her disability that, for the last ten years of her life, she had been almost totally dependent on her husband, who would carry her from one room to another when she became incapable of walking.

After her death, Doughty married Edith, the former district nurse of Church Stretton and, by all accounts, was a devoted husband. When Kathleen, his only child, was born two years later, she was the light of her father's life and he spent every minute of his spare time with her. The little family seemed perfectly content, so much so that John Doughty rarely left the house except to attend church on Sundays.

On the morning of the murder of his wife and daughter, John Doughty had breakfasted with the Doughty's lodger, Miss Emily Tait, who worked at a nearby café. Edith and Kathleen were still asleep in bed and, when Miss Tait left to go to work at just before half-past eight, John Doughty seemed to her to be his normal self. He was seen visiting the post office 100 yards from his home shortly afterwards, then nothing was seen or heard of any members of the family until Doughty was discovered in the backyard at around nine o'clock. When police questioned neighbours and passers-by, they could find no evidence of any strangers in the area at the time of the murders and neither could they find anyone who could suggest any reason at all why such a quiet, inoffensive and seemingly devoted family man should suddenly kill his wife and daughter and then attempt to take his own life.

A postcard of Church Stretton. (Author's collection)

Church Stretton, 1960s.
(Author's collection)

However, when police searched the house, they found more than 100 unopened letters, many of which were either unpaid bills or final demands for payment. It appeared that John Doughty was in debt by about £100, a sum that would equate today to several thousand pounds. Apparently, Doughty had been driven almost mad with worry about his ever-increasing debts and his consequent inability to provide for the family he loved and in his mind, the only possible solution to his financial problems was to eliminate first his family, then himself, to avoid the shame of possible bankruptcy.

Sixty-four-year-old Doughty first appeared before magistrates at Church Stretton only days after the murder, conveyed to court wrapped in a blanket on a stretcher, which was laid before the magistrate's table. Throughout the proceedings, Doughty lay immobile on his back, staring resolutely at the ceiling and adding nothing to his only real statement to date, which was, 'I don't remember doing it'. He was remanded in custody.

By his final appearance at the magistrate's court, Doughty was able to sit upright supported by two warders, one at each side. Dressed in a grey suit covered by a darker overcoat, the elderly man stared resolutely at the floor as the various witnesses testified. Occasionally, he buried his head in his hands and sobbed quietly.

The magistrate's heard how Doughty had complained of suffering severe pains in his head for several weeks before the murder. The pain usually woke him in the early hours of the morning and he described them as being like a wheel of fire going round and round in front of him. He could recall little of the events of 24 October – in fact practically his only memory was of lying in the yard and hearing someone say, 'Give him some brandy.'

The magistrates had no authority to consider Doughty's mental state at the time of the murder and, since a coroner's jury had already recorded two counts of wilful murder against him, they had no option but to commit him for trial at the next Shropshire Assizes. There he was found 'Guilty, but insane' and ordered to be detained as a criminal lunatic at His Majesty's pleasure.

23

'HE WAS A VERY NAUGHTY BOY'

Market Drayton, 1936

Domestic servant Dorothy Clewes, from Grotto Road, Market Drayton, was a popular girl, particularly with the town's young men. That said, she was a rather cautious young woman and chose her friends carefully – unfortunately, in choosing to go out with local farm labourer Ernest Robert Hill, she made a mistake that would ultimately cost her life.

Dorothy and Ernest had been 'walking out' together for almost a year and had become engaged at Christmas 1935. However, by Easter 1936, Dorothy was beginning to tire of Ernest's affections. Eighteen-year-old Ernest's love for Dorothy was almost obsessive and he lived in constant fear that the pretty, vivacious girl would be unfaithful to him.

His insecurity and constant accusations came to a head on Good Friday, when Ernest told Dorothy that he believed that she had been for a walk with another man. Dorothy had done no such thing and, when she protested as much to Ernest, he grabbed her arm in a fit of jealous rage and squeezed it so tightly that it left bruises in the shape of his fingers on her flesh. For Dorothy, this act of unprovoked violence was the last straw and she immediately told Ernest that their relationship was over. Ernest had no intention of letting Dorothy go without a fight. He begged and pleaded for another chance, but Dorothy was adamant.

In a small place like Market Drayton, it was impossible for the couple to avoid bumping into each other and, on 13 April, Easter Monday, Ernest spotted eighteen-year-old Dorothy in the town. To his horror, he saw that Dorothy was wearing lipstick and a touch of face powder, giving every appearance of being dressed up to go on a date. When Ernest's friends told him that Dorothy already had another

Grotto Road, Market Drayton. (© N. Sly, 2008)

boyfriend, an RAF airman, the young man found himself seized by an overpowering fit of jealousy.

Later that same day, Dorothy went for a walk with her sister, Florrie, and a friend, Phyllis Garratt. The weather was warm and sunny and the girls casually sauntered along the road between Market Drayton and Tern Hill, chatting companionably. They were about 1½ miles outside Market Drayton when a cyclist suddenly came up behind them and overtook them. As he passed the girls, the cyclist looked back over his shoulder, glaring directly at Dorothy. It was Ernest Hill.

Hill continued for about 50 yards before dismounting and propping his bicycle against a tree. As the girls approached him, he stepped into the road in front of them, one hand tucked inside his mackintosh coat. Looking directly at Dorothy, he calmly said 'Hello'. Then, without saying another word, he pulled a sawn-off shotgun out of his coat and aimed it at Dorothy's heart, holding the gun so close to her that it actually touched the material on the front of her coat.

'Don't be so stupid,' Florrie told Hill and, grabbing her sister's arm, she tried to pull her out of the way. As she did so, there was a loud bang, at which all three girls ran off up the road. Hill calmly replaced his gun inside his coat, mounted his bicycle and rode off without speaking.

A postcard of the Butter Cross at Market Drayton, 1950s. (Author's collection)

The road from Market Drayton to Tern Hill as it is today. (© R. Sly, 2008)

Dorothy had been shot in her left upper arm and the gun had been so close that, when fired, it set light to her dress. Florrie and Phyllis quickly put out the flames then Phyllis ran to nearby cottages for help, while Florrie comforted her sister, trying to staunch the flow of blood from her arm with her handkerchief.

Dorothy was taken into a cottage, where a dressing was applied to her wounds. A passing motorist was sent to fetch the police, who immediately rushed Dorothy to the cottage hospital at Market Drayton in a police car. At the hospital, surgeons removed ninety-nine shotgun pellets from her arm. Although she was very shocked and in considerable pain, it was thought that Dorothy's wounds were not life threatening and she was described by the hospital as being in a 'stable condition' after her ordeal.

Local constable PC Fred Jones immediately went to interview Hill, who freely admitted to shooting his former fiancée. When PC Jones searched the jacket that Hill had been wearing, the gun was still in an inside pocket. It seemed an open and shut case and Hill was arrested and taken into custody, pending a hearing before the local magistrates.

Although she had initially appeared to be recovering in hospital, Dorothy's condition suddenly and unexpectedly took a turn for the worse. When it became apparent that she was gravely ill, a deposition was taken from they dying girl, in which she stated that Hill had shot her. Dorothy died on 23 April and, having carried out a post-mortem examination on her body, Dr Edgar Conningsby Myott determined the cause of her death to be tetanus.

The charge against Ernest Hill was now elevated to one of wilful murder and, while Hill continued to admit to the shooting, he now maintained that he had intended only to frighten Dorothy by firing into the air rather than to hurt her.

Hill was committed for trial at the Shrewsbury Assizes on 27 June, before Mr Justice Porter. He pleaded 'Not Guilty' to the murder of Dorothy Clewes, but the

Market Drayton Cottage Hospital. (© R. Sly, 2008)

prosecution reminded the jury of his confession to PC Jones on his arrest and placed great emphasis on the fact that, prior to the shooting, Hill had collected the gun from his aunt's home, where it had been kept for many years, then deliberately visited a local blacksmith in order to have the barrels sawn off, making it easier to conceal.

The defence pointed out that Dorothy had actually died from tetanus and, although she obviously would not have contracted it had she not been shot, the actual shotgun wound was a comparatively minor injury. The standard of care at the local cottage hospital was questioned, particularly the fact that Dorothy had not been given an injection of anti-tetanus serum as part of her treatment. To support this argument, the defence called Dr James Aubrey Ireland, a physician and surgeon, who had practised for thirty-one years. Ireland testified that, where shooting injuries were concerned, it was considered standard practice to administer an anti-tetanus serum, since the gunshot wounds provided an excellent entrance point for the tetanus bacilli.

A letter that had been found in Hill's pocket on his arrest was read out in court:

Dear Doll, just a few lines to wish you all the happiness in the world. I don't know where I am going, but that doesn't matter to you now. You can't believe me and you don't really want me. So I may as well go and never come back. I must say I am sorry for the way I have treated you; rather badly, I know, but only in fun, but you forgave me. Please don't worry about me. I shall be alright. So I must leave you now. Goodbye, Dolly, with all my love. [*sic*]

Hill's defence lawyer, Mr Cartwright Sharp, asked the jury if this was really the letter of a man who was intending to kill the recipient.

The defence maintained that Hill's only intention had been to frighten Dorothy and that the gun had gone off accidentally. Mr Cartwright Sharp described the shooting as a 'rash moment' and a 'boyish act of folly', admitting that firing the gun was a ridiculous thing to do, but stressing that Hill was 'only a child.' He had been wearing heavy gloves at the time that the shot was fired and tests had shown that the gun required only a pressure of 2½lb to fire, as opposed to a more normal 5lb.

If there was one thing that was clear about this case, it was that Hill was absolutely devoted to Dorothy. 'He was a very naughty boy', Cartwright Sharp told the jury.

Mr St J.G. Micklethwaite, acting for the prosecution, disagreed. Urging the jury, 'Don't let your sympathy for the living obliterate your memory for the dead.' He reminded them that Hill had gone to considerable trouble to retrieve the gun from his aunt's home and have it modified. If he had not intended to hurt Dorothy, why had he been carrying the gun in the first place and, more importantly, why had he loaded it? Hill had initially aimed the gun directly at Dorothy's heart and, had her sister not pulled her away, the shot would almost certainly have hit her there rather than in her arm. The cause of Dorothy's death might have been tetanus, but if she hadn't been shot then she wouldn't have contracted the disease, making her death a direct result of the shooting.

The judge summarised the case, paying particular attention to the legal differences between murder and manslaughter. The jury retired for ninety minutes, taking the gun and Hill's gloves with them into the deliberation room, and returned with a verdict of 'Guilty', although they added a recommendation of mercy. There was momentary chaos in the courtroom as Hill's mother immediately fainted on hearing the verdict and a female juror was also overcome with emotion. When order had been restored, Mr Justice Porter passed the death sentence on Ernest Robert Hill.

An appeal was lodged against the sentence on the grounds that Mr Justice Porter's summary of the case had been unsatisfactory, particularly with regard to the testimony of Florrie Clewes and Phyllis Garratt, who had naturally given eyewitness accounts of the shooting. On 13 July, Mr Justice Goddard ruled that Porter's summing up was entirely accurate and that he had made certain that he had explained the difference between murder and manslaughter to the jury. The appeal was therefore dismissed. However, on 20 July 1936, the Home Secretary recommended a reprieve and Hill's death sentence was commuted to one of life imprisonment.

24

'I HAVE NOTHING TO SAY'

Butcher Charlie Wells was beginning to feel a little concerned about his delivery driver, William Bufton. Thirty-two-year-old Bufton had set off earlier that day on his usual round, which covered the small town of Clun and its surrounding areas, most of which were rural and hence quite isolated. Now, with Bufton's expected return to the shop long overdue, Wells began to wonder if his van had broken down, leaving him stranded miles from anywhere.

Wells and his son got into their own van and began to trace Bufton's most likely route. However, rather than finding the delivery man's van broken down at the roadside as they had expected, it was neatly parked outside the home of Mr and Mrs Venables at Pen-y-Wern.

Wells knew that Bufton was on friendly terms with both Mr and Mrs Venables and that he often stopped at their home for a welcome cup of tea while delivering their meat order. Mr Venables worked as a farm labourer and, each day would cycle to and from work, a distance of 12 miles. His fifty-two-year-old wife, Martha, was a housewife and, living in an isolated cottage, was always ready to welcome visitors to her home, pleased to have a bit of company. There was nothing remotely untoward about the friendship between the housewife and the delivery driver, who was, after all, twenty years her junior. Indeed, on the occasions when Mr Venables was not working, he too welcomed Bufton's visits.

Even having traced William Bufton's van to the home of a regular customer, Wells still felt uneasy. Bufton should have delivered to the Venables household and left there several hours previously. Anxiously, Wells knocked at the front door of the cottage and called out, but there was no reply.

Pen-y-Wern. (© N. Sly, 2008)

Telling his son to wait for him in the van, Wells walked round the side of the cottage to the back and began peering through the windows. To his horror, through the kitchen window, he spotted Martha Venables lying on the floor, half underneath the table.

Wells ran back to the locked front door and managed to shoulder his way into the house. In the kitchen, he found that there were not one, but two bodies lying under the table. Martha Jane Venables and William Gerrard Frank Bufton had both been shot and, such was the severity of their wounds that both would almost certainly have died instantly. Bufton had been shot in the face and the force of the shot had blown much of his head clean off his body. Martha Venables had a large wound in her chest and abdomen, which exposed her internal organs.

The police were summoned, along with a doctor, although the doctor could do little for Bufton and Mrs Venables other than pronounce them dead. It was immediately obvious that their deaths had been the result of foul play, since no gun was found on the premises. Therefore someone must have shot them and then left the cottage, taking the murder weapon with him or her. More puzzling to the police was finding any possible motive for the murder. Nothing had been stolen from the cottage and Bufton's van was still parked outside, its contents untouched.

The police interviewed the owners of the few properties at Pen-y-Wern and discovered that Bufton had delivered to a nearby cottage at 1.55 p.m. and, shortly afterwards, had been seen arriving at the home of Mr and Mrs Venables. Two shots, fired in quick succession, had been heard at about 2.15 p.m., but nobody had seen anything unusual or noted the presence of any strangers in the area.

In the midst of their investigations at Pen-y-Wern, the police were called away urgently to a house at Woodside, Clun, where a man had apparently attempted suicide. George Owen had cut his own throat and was taken to hospital at Shrewsbury, where the relatively minor wound was stitched up. Until the passing of the 1961 Suicide Act in England, committing or attempting to commit suicide was a criminal offence and, as this was 1939, it was routine for Owen to be interviewed by the police. Surprisingly, Owen initially denied that his throat wound was self-inflicted, telling the police that it had been done earlier that afternoon by butcher's boy William Bufton.

As soon as Owen mentioned Bufton, the police had a suspect for the double murder. A check with doctors at the hospital confirmed that Owen's throat had been slashed by his own hand and, when his clothing was searched, the police found three women's handkerchiefs in the pocket of his jacket, one of which was identical to one known to have been owned by Martha Venables. The police moved to search Owen's house where they found a shotgun, which had recently been fired. They also found two spent cartridges on the road between Pen-y-Wern and Woodside and experts would later determine that those cartridges had been fired from the gun found at Owen's house.

A postcard of Clun. (Author's collection)

Clun today. (© N. Sly, 2008)

While Owen was recovering from his injuries in hospital, the police thoroughly investigated both his background and his movements on 28 June, the day of the double murder.

Owen was known to be under a considerable amount of strain. His wife was a chronic invalid and, as well as working to support his family, Owen bore much of the responsibility for her day-to-day care and that of the couple's children. As a consequence, he had recently become very depressed and had made numerous threats to take his own life. In addition, he had an intense dislike of William Bufton, to whom he was related by marriage, and had been heard to threaten to kill him or shoot him on more than one occasion.

As she had with William Bufton, Martha Venables often welcomed George Owen as a visitor into her home. Owen worked as a roadman and, whenever he was working in the vicinity of her cottage, used an outbuilding there to store his tools. He had also eaten his lunch at the cottage and been given cups of tea.

A witness, insurance agent Derek Horton George, came forward to say that he had seen Owen working close to the scene of the murders at 1.10 p.m. on 28 June, a sighting that was evidenced by piles of freshly-cut gorse in the immediate area.

The police arrested George Owen on his release from hospital and, on 1 August 1939, charged him with attempted suicide and with the wilful murders of Martha Venables and William Bufton. When Superintendent J.H. Machin of the Shropshire County Constabulary at Ludlow read out the charges against him, George Owen simply responded, 'I have nothing to say.'

Clun. (© N. Sly, 2008)

Owen initially continued to deny any involvement in the killings, telling the police that he had borrowed the shotgun from a friend with the intention of killing rabbits. Yet, even as he was denying the murders, Owen expressed a vehement and totally irrational hatred for William Bufton, the husband of his niece, who he claimed was an idle parasite, who spent too much time drinking tea when he should have been out delivering meat. Eventually, Owen was to make a full confession.

He was committed by magistrates to stand trial at the Shropshire Assizes, although by the time his trial opened in November 1939, his mental state had deteriorated to such an extent that he was deemed 'unfit to plead'. The presiding judge, Mr Justice Lawrence, therefore had no alternative but to order that he be detained at His Majesty's pleasure.

[Note: In some contemporary accounts of the murder, the forename of victim Mrs Venables is recorded as Jennifer.]

The grave of William Bufton, Clun. (© N. Sly, 2008)

25

'HE WILL CATCH HIS DEATH OF COLD'

Minsterley, 1945

Life had treated Dennis O'Neill cruelly. By 1945, the thirteen-year-old boy from Newport in Monmouthshire had been in the care of Newport County Council for six years, as had his younger brothers, Terence and Frederick. However, in June 1944, it appeared as if a suitable foster family had finally been found for the boy and he was sent to live with farmer Reginald Gough and his wife, Esther, at Minsterley. Terence joined him there two weeks later. Dennis's feelings on his foster placement are not recorded. Perhaps he saw it as a new beginning – a chance to become part of a loving family. Maybe he was anxious and apprehensive. He certainly could never have envisaged the way his new life would ultimately turn out.

On 9 January 1945, Esther Gough overslept and didn't get up until nine o'clock in the morning. She initially recalled the events of the rest of the morning as follows: Having lit the fire, she called to Terence to get up, telling Dennis, who had been unwell the night before, to stay in bed a while longer. Terence came downstairs for his breakfast complaining of feeling tired and telling Mrs Gough that he and his brother had been fighting during the night and that Dennis hadn't let him sleep.

After breakfast, Terence was sent to feed some horses on the farm and Esther went upstairs to ask Dennis if he wanted a cup of tea. He said that he would like one, so she made him some and took it up to his room. However, when she got there, Dennis appeared to have fallen asleep again, so she left the tea in his room and went back downstairs again. While first in his bedroom, she had noticed that Dennis had some red marks on his chest, which he said were due to Terence scratching him.

Esther Gough went back to the boys' bedroom a little while later, this time with a cup of hot milk for Dennis. Again, Dennis seemed too drowsy to drink, so she left him to sleep. Then, at about half-past eleven, she heard noises coming from upstairs. When she checked, she found Dennis stumbling around, completely naked. Esther called her husband who carried Dennis back to bed and sent his wife to a neighbour, Mrs Millage, who had a telephone.

Esther arrived at Mrs Millage's house at about one o'clock and asked her to please ring for a doctor as a young boy living with them was having a fit. By the time Dr Holloway Davies reached the isolated farmhouse at three o'clock that afternoon, Dennis had, in his estimation, been dead for between four and six hours and, horrified by the boy's condition, Dr Davies immediately informed both the coroner and the police of his findings.

At a post-mortem examination, carried out the following day by Dr A.J. Rhodes, a pathologist at the Royal Salop Infirmary, it was found that Dennis was severely undernourished, thin and wasted. He was 3in shorter than would normally be expected at his age and weighed almost 1½ stones less than the normal weight for a thirteen-year-old boy. His feet and legs were covered in septic ulcers and his legs were severely chapped. There were numerous fresh bruises on both his chest and back. Dr Rhodes determined that Dennis had been violently beaten on his chest and back and, in his weakened and malnourished state, had succumbed to heart failure. The chronic sepsis of his legs had been a contributory factor, although it in itself had not been sufficiently advanced to cause the boy's death.

The dirty bedroom where Dennis had been found was almost completely bare of furniture and, even though the weather was cold and there was snow on the

Minsterley. (© N. Sly, 2008)

ground outside, had no heating. There were no rugs or carpet on the floor and the barren room contained just an iron bedstead, a palliasse and a flock mattress.

Police Sergeant Macpherson immediately interviewed Mrs Gough, who told him that Dennis had been small for his age when he first arrived to live with them, but he had always had a good appetite and ate well. Just before Christmas, he and Terence had both complained of having chilblains on their feet, which Mrs Gough had been treating with healing ointment and bandages. Dennis's feet had become discoloured and the skin on them had broken and, just after Christmas, he began to say that his feet hurt all the time and that he couldn't stand up properly. Mrs Gough had told him that she would fetch the doctor, but said that Dennis had insisted that he was all right.

On the night before his death, Mrs Gough said that Dennis had fallen down a number of times and her husband had eventually carried him off to bed before starting the evening milking. Dennis and Terence had been fighting together during that night. Mrs Gough's story of the morning of his death had slightly changed. She told the policeman that she had taken drinks to Dennis in bed. Then she and her husband had gone to fetch groceries and, when they returned, her husband had gone to check on Dennis and found him unconscious. He had sent her to the neighbours to call the doctor, who had been out when she rang.

Esther Gough explained the lack of bedclothes in the boys' room by saying that both boys regularly wet and soiled their bedding. Since Dennis had been at the farm, she had occasionally hit him on the hand with a stick for misbehaviour. She had never hit him on the back or the chest. She was aware that he had marks on his back but believed those to result from a fall downstairs on the day before he died. She attributed the other bruises on Dennis's body to fights between him and his brother.

Reginald Gough's statement to the police matched his wife's almost exactly. However Terence, who was naturally immediately removed from the Gough's home, had a different story to tell.

Terence told the police that he and his brother had been thrashed nightly ever since their arrival at the farm. Every evening they were expected to tell Mr Gough what they had done wrong during that day and he gave them 'stripes' on the hand for every wrongdoing, often as much as ten stripes for one thing. Sometimes they had a hundred stripes a night and at other times they were thrashed on their legs.

The two boys had very often been hungry and were in the habit of sneaking into the pantry to steal food. Although they were never actually caught in the act, the Goughs always found out and punished them, usually with stripes on their hands. Dennis, in particular, had often been punished by being refused food and had, on occasions, suckled the teats of the Gough's milking cows in order to pacify his hunger and obtain some nourishment.

Once, Dennis was sent to a spinney to gather sticks and had not collected enough. Mrs Gough had chased him with a stick, thrown her heavy clogs at him and pulled him back to the spinney by his hair. He believed that it was on the same day that Dennis had gone into the yard to wash his hands at the pump. Mr Gough had come into the house saying that Dennis had jumped into the trough and Gough had then stripped off Dennis's clothes and thrashed him with a stick.

On the night before his brother died, Terence had been sent to bed early, leaving his brother standing naked and cold in the kitchen. That day, the ravenously hungry Dennis had taken a bite from a swede in the cowshed and, as a punishment for this, Mr Gough had tied him to a pig bench in the back kitchen with a rope. Mr Gough had then thrashed the boy's back with a stick. Terence had heard Dennis crying downstairs and, when he finally came to bed, he was still naked. During that night, Mr Gough had come into their bedroom, enraged because Dennis would not stop crying. According to Terence, Mr Gough had knelt on the bed and thumped Dennis very hard on his chest with both fists.

Reginald Gough, aged thirty-one, and twenty-nine-year-old Esther were charged with the manslaughter of Dennis O'Neill by neglect and violence. After appearing before magistrates at Pontesbury, they were committed for trial at the next assizes.

Their trial opened at Stafford on 15 March 1945, before Mr Justice Wrottesley and a host of prosecution and defence counsels. Mr W.H. Cartwright Sharp KC and Mr H.H. Maddocks prosecuted the case, while Mr and Mrs Gough both retained separate defence counsels. Mr W. Field Hunt represented Newport Corporation, while Norman Carr represented Shropshire County Council. Both Reginald and Esther Gough pleaded 'Not Guilty' to the charges against them.

The prosecution maintained that, having care and custody of Dennis, Mr and Mrs Gough had brought about his death by cruelty and neglect. The court was told that no possible naughtiness on the part of a child could excuse beating him with a stick until he bled and nothing could justify punching him with a fist so that he was badly bruised.

The court heard from Miss Eirlys Edwards, who visited foster homes on behalf of the Newport Education Committee. She had last seen Terence and Dennis on 20 December 1944 and had noticed that Dennis seemed very pale and nervous. She spoke to both boys, who had told her that they were perfectly happy and liked being there. Nevertheless, Miss Edwards had sensed that something was not quite right. She told Mrs Gough that Dennis must see a doctor, saying that the Education Authority would pay. Mrs Gough had promised to call a doctor for Dennis, but had not done so.

Miss Edwards, who was young and inexperienced, had been visiting the farm only to discuss arrangements for paying the Gough's their allowance for caring for the two boys. There had been some dispute between the Newport Education Authority and Shropshire Council, since Newport's rates of payment for fostering were higher than those generally given by authorities in Shropshire. Because of this, Shropshire Council had written to the Newport authorities saying that they felt unable to supervise their cases.

Still, Miss Edwards knew that things weren't as they should be at the Gough's farm. She had submitted written reports to both the Newport and Shropshire authorities, recommending the immediate removal of the boys from the Gough's care and stressing that she had several times impressed upon Mrs Gough the need for Dennis to be seen by a doctor. Her reports had been shelved over the Christmas period, waiting for people to return from their holidays and take action on them.

Dr Rhodes and Dr Davies both testified about Dennis's appalling medical condition, then Reginald Gough was called to the stand. He repeated his statement to the police of finding the boy stumbling about naked on the stairs on the morning of his death and carrying him to bed then sending his wife to call a doctor. Gough denied that Dennis had already been dead when the doctor was finally summoned. He admitted that his wife had a very heavy workload on the farm, but denied being jealous of any affection that she showed the boys. 'There was always plenty of food for them,' he said before finally stepping down.

The court then heard from Bob Smith, a road worker who occasionally lodged at the Gough's farm. He had spent the weekend before Dennis's death at the farm and had noticed nothing unusual about the boy.

It was then Esther Gough's turn to give evidence. Esther told the court that she had worked in service from the age of fourteen until she had joined the WAAF in June 1941, serving until January 1942, when she was discharged. She had met Reginald in December 1941 and married him the following February. The couple had no children of their own.

Mrs Gough told the court that, as well as having day-to-day care of the foster children and doing all of the housework and the cooking, she was also expected to help out on the farm. Her regular duties included helping at milking, cleaning the cow house, looking after 100 chickens and twenty ducks and feeding the calves. Terence had occasionally helped her around the house and, on one occasion, had kissed her goodnight. This display of affection from the child had sent her husband into a fit of jealousy. He had first sulked and refused to speak to her then later shouted and cursed at her, finally hitting her.

When she married her husband in 1942, Esther Gough told the court that she had believed that she loved him. However, she had very quickly come to fear him. Such was her fear of her husband that she had actually chosen to stay in prison while awaiting her trial and had refused the bail that she had been offered on 22 February.

By August 1942, Esther Gough had been diagnosed by a doctor as suffering from nervous debility caused by the strain of her home life. She left her husband and on 6 August 1942 applied for a separation order on the grounds of persistent cruelty. The case had been referred to a probation officer and resulted in Gough being convicted of common assault. Yet, for reasons known only to herself, Esther Gough had then returned to live with her husband.

Speaking of Dennis's death, Esther Gough seemed distressed. She was handed a glass of water and allowed to sit down while she told the court that, on the night before his death, Dennis had been beaten by her husband and made to stand naked outside in the yard. She had remonstrated with her husband saying;

'He will catch his death of cold', at which Reginald had brought the boy indoors. She had seen her husband hitting the boy on both sides of his head and punching him on his chest and back.

Esther said that she had told her husband to leave the boy alone and that Reginald had eventually carried Dennis to bed. On the following morning, she had not taken drinks to Dennis's bedroom as she had first stated, but instead had been told by her husband that the boy was dead. Reginald ordered her to 'phone for the doctor and to say that the boy was unconscious after having had a fit.'

Terence O'Neill was called to the witness stand and his testimony took over three hours. He spoke of regular beatings and starvation and of Dennis being locked in closets or shut outside. Yet he also talked of happier times – of Mr and Mrs Gough listening to them saying their prayers at night and playing cricket and football with them. He admitted that he and Dennis were often naughty and that they sometimes deserved to be punished. He also admitted engaging in physical fights with his brother, which the Gough's had tried to prevent.

At the conclusion of the case, Mr Justice Wrottesley told the jury that, as far as the case of manslaughter was concerned, they could not fairly find Mrs Gough guilty, since her husband was the only person who could have caused the marks on Dennis. However, to find Reginald Gough not guilty of manslaughter, they would have to disbelieve the evidence of Mrs Gough, Terence O'Neill and the medical witnesses.

As far as the case of manslaughter was concerned, Mrs Gough was clearly not an accomplice, but the jury must ask themselves whether or not she was an accomplice in the matter of neglect.

The jury retired for twenty minutes, returning with a verdict of 'Guilty of manslaughter' against Reginald Gough and 'Guilty of neglect' against his wife.

Esther was sentenced to six months imprisonment, while Reginald received a sentence of six years penal servitude for his part in Dennis O'Neill's tragic death.

Reginald Gough's light sentence caused a public outcry and his conviction was later re-examined and upgraded to one for murder. He received an additional four years sentence, which was still widely thought to be far too lenient, given his prolonged maltreatment of, and cruelty to, his foster child.

In April 1945, the government requested Sir Walter Monckton KC to make an enquiry into the case. Monckton highlighted a number of failings in the system for dealing with foster children, including a serious lack of supervision by the local authority, poor record keeping and filing, lack of inter-agency cooperation, staff shortages, and 'a lamentable failure of communication.' The Goughs had apparently been selected as foster parents without adequate checks first being made into their suitability and had received very little supervision during the time Dennis and Terence were in their care.

Shropshire County Council also set up a sub-committee to investigate matters arising from the tragic case and agreed to implement several measures to try and prevent a recurrence in the future. While accepting the main criticisms of the

Monckton report, the council was at pains to point out that, due to the war, they were experiencing severe staffing difficulties. 'The existing system of dealing with boarded-out children has failed to prevent a tragedy and a thorough reorganisation is called for', stated the council's report.

Sadly, the investigations and recommendations came too late to save Dennis O'Neill, who had endured unimaginable cruelty at the hands of a man who, just months before, had signed a declaration which read:

I, Reginald Gough, do hereby engage with the local authority of Newport in consideration of my receiving a sum of £1 per week to bring up Dennis O'Neill aged 13 as one of my own children and to provide him with proper food, lodgings and washing and to endeavour to train him in the habits of honesty, obedience, personal cleanliness and industry and to take care that he will duly attend at church and at school. I do further undertake that I will provide for the proper repair and renewal of his clothing and in case of his illness, I shall report forthwith to the above authority and shall permit him at all times to be examined and the home and clothing to be inspected by any inspector appointed by the authority.

26

'THE MONEY WON'T DO YOU ANY GOOD, MY LAD'

Ketley, 1950

John Edge lived at The Queen's Head public house at Ketley with his seventy-four-year-old mother, Jane, who had been the licensee for twenty-two years. John worked at Hadley, at the Sankey Castle Works, and every morning would leave the pub to catch his bus at about twenty minutes past six, having first taken his mother a cup of tea in bed.

Jane usually got up at about eight o'clock, by which time her daily help, Mrs Shotton, had arrived. Most mornings, she would go into Wellington to do some shopping, returning in time to open up the pub at half past ten. Lunchtimes were invariably quiet – sometimes there would be no customers at all and there would rarely be more than four or five drinkers for her to serve. Most of the pub's business was done in the evenings, by which time John had returned from work and was able to lend a hand.

On 6 September 1950, the day started as normal. Jane served a handful of customers at lunchtime and was seen outside the pub by a neighbour at around twenty past two in the afternoon. However, when John arrived home at between a quarter and half past five, unusually the front door of the pub was locked. John let himself in through the side door and went to the private quarters of the pub where he found his mother sitting in an easy chair, her Pekingese dog by her side.

At first, he thought his mother was simply dozing, her head tilted slightly to one side, but, as he moved forward to wake her, he realised that she had suffered terrible head injuries and was actually dead.

John called for a doctor and Dr John Sheehan, from Sefton General Hospital in Liverpool, who was doing locum duties in Wellington, arrived at about ten past six. There was nothing he could do to help Mrs Edge who had apparently been dead for at least two hours.

At first, everything in the pub and its living quarters looked perfectly normal. None of the furniture had been disarranged and nothing seemed to have been disturbed. A pan of peeled potatoes in cold water stood on the stove ready to be cooked and a teapot with dry tealeaves waited by the sink for someone to add boiling water. On finding his mother dead, John Edge immediately went to a neighbour's house for assistance and, as he walked through the pub to go outside, he saw nothing out of the ordinary. Only when he returned did he notice that the drawer had been removed from the pub till and lay empty on the bar counter. Later still, John found that some of his mother's jewellery was missing, including a gold wristwatch, a gold bracelet, a gold chain with a spade guinea on it and an artificial pearl necklace. A pint mug containing pound notes was still untouched on a shelf behind the bar, even though it was in plain view.

The police were called and, later that evening, a post-mortem examination was conducted. Professor J.M. Webster, the director of the Home Office Laboratory in Birmingham, went first to the Queen's Head then supervised the removal of Jane Edge's body to the mortuary at Wellington. Webster listed a catalogue of injuries to the old woman, mainly bruises, abrasions, scratches and lacerations

A postcard of Wellington. (Author's collection)

to her head and face. Mrs Edge had not been in the best of health before she was attacked. Webster found that she had an enlarged heart and suggested that her blood pressure had most probably been raised. She was also suffering from chronic bronchitis. Fear at being attacked would have put an enormous strain on her heart and Webster concluded that Mrs Edge had been hit on the head and also grasped by the throat, after which she had died from a combination of shock and heart failure. In the course of his examination, Webster also determined that Mrs Edge's blood was Group A.

Having subjected the entire premises to a fingertip search, the police began their investigations by appealing for anyone who had visited the pub at lunchtime on 6 September to come forward. Percy Archer and Alfred Pugh both gave interviews. Neither man had seen anything suspicious, although Archer did tell the police that he had passed the pub at about three o'clock in the afternoon and noticed that the back door was open. Pugh told the investigating officers that he had spent about three quarters of an hour at the pub, leaving at about 1.45 p.m. There had been three other customers in the bar, two of whom were obviously Percy Archer and his nephew, who was drinking with him. Pugh had not recognised the third man. When he left the pub, Mrs Edge had followed him outside to shake some crumbs off a tablecloth. A dustman, Thomas Price, told the police that at 3.40 p.m. he had passed the pub while on his rounds and had glimpsed a man inside through a window. Although he hadn't seen the man's face, he described him as being of a similar build to John Edge. He had also heard Mrs Edge's dog barking.

The police began conducting house-to-house enquiries in the neighbourhood and, by 7 September, had reached the Apley Industrial Hostel, where they spoke to manager Bertie Juggins in his office. The office adjoined a bedroom rented by forty-year-old labourer Frank Griffin, and, during the course of the interview, Juggins opened the door to see if Griffin was in.

He wasn't and Juggins gave the police officers permission to search the room. In a chest of drawers, they found a cream coloured shirt, which appeared to be bloodstained at the front on the right-hand side. They also found a Gladstone bag, which contained a large quantity of copper and silver coins.

Bertie Juggins next saw Griffin in a public house at lunchtime on 8 September. Griffin bought Juggins a drink and asked him to make up his account as he was intending to leave the hostel. He also told Juggins that he was going to see the police. At six o'clock that evening, Griffin settled his bill, telling Juggins that the police had finished with him and that he was going to Birmingham.

Before leaving, Griffin paid off some outstanding debts. He visited cycle-dealer William Perry, from whom he had previously obtained a £1 loan, leaving a suitcase as security. Now he reclaimed his case, giving Perry 25s in exchange. He asked Perry if he could change still more coins for notes, and Perry counted out £5's worth of silver and gave Griffin five £1 notes. 'Remember. I have not been here tonight – you haven't seen me,' Griffin mysteriously told Perry and his wife before leaving.

Griffin only got as far as the Tontine Hotel in Ironbridge, arriving there at about seven o'clock on the evening of 8 September. After drinking a beer and a double whisky in the bar, he asked landlord, John Rowley, if there was a bus to Kidderminster that night. Rowley told him that the last bus had already left, so Griffin asked him to order a taxi for him. It arrived at about 7.45 p.m.

However, Griffin was back at the Tontine Hotel early the following morning, asking for a room, which he booked in the name of Jenkins, telling Mr Rowley that he came from Birmingham. Claiming to be very tired, he asked Mr Rowley for a half-bottle of Scotch to take to his room. Rowley was unable to supply one, so even though it was before eight o'clock in the morning, Griffin drank a double Scotch at the bar, and then went to his room with half a bottle of gin. He didn't reappear until that evening, when he purchased a second half-bottle of gin.

By now, Rowley's suspicions were aroused and he telephoned the police, who arrived at the hotel at midday on Sunday 10 September. Rowley went up to Griffin's room to tell him that the police wanted a word, to which Griffin replied that he would come right down. When he hadn't appeared after fifteen minutes, Rowley escorted the two policemen up to his room.

PC France, one of the officers, introduced himself and his colleague PC Reeves to the room's occupant, who told him that he was Mr Jenkins. France told the man that he knew that his name was Frank Griffin, but Griffin nervously denied it, keeping up the pretence for several minutes, all the while continuing to drink his gin.

France asked 'Mr Jenkins' if he had ever been in the Queen's Head at Ketley. The man was silent for a while then he suddenly slumped onto his bed and began to sob noisily. 'It wasn't worth it,' he said. 'I did not get much. She fell down.'

Griffin was cautioned, but went on to make a statement, which PC France wrote down. Trembling convulsively, Griffin told the officers that he had hit Mrs Edge over the head with a pint mug, and then taken the contents of the till and some jewellery.

At 2.45 p.m., PC France asked Griffin to sign the statement that he had written. Griffin took the pen and was poised to sign the statement when he suddenly collapsed, the pen trailing a line across the constable's notebook. Griffin was half carried from the hotel and taken to Ironbridge police station. Later that evening, the statement was read out to him, but now Griffin refused to sign it, claiming to have been drunk when he made it.

Griffin was taken by car to Wellington police station. He was later to claim that, during the course of the journey, he asked the police for a drink. Superintendent Rudkin stopped the car and bought two half bottles of gin, which he then allowed Griffin to drink throughout his interview. Hence, Griffin insisted, he could not recall anything he had said at Wellington.

The story that he told the police at Wellington was that he had been drinking heavily that morning. He remembered visiting the Lamb public house then could recall absolutely nothing until he woke up at seven o'clock that evening at the Apley Hostel.

Griffin was charged with the wilful murder of Jane Edge and committed by magistrates to stand trial at the Shropshire Assizes. The trial opened before Mr Justice Cassels on 20 November 1950, with John Foster and Mr W. Field Hunt prosecuting. Griffin was granted Legal Aid for his defence, which was handled by A.J. Long and G.K. Mynett.

After pleading 'Not Guilty', Griffin listened dispassionately as the prosecution introduced a number of witnesses to testify against him. It emerged that ashes had been removed from the grate in his room at the Apley Hostel, which, when tested, were believed to have been the burned remains of Mrs Edge's artificial pearl necklace. Also found among the ashes was a piece of paper, on which there was a small amount of Group A blood. The cream shirt retrieved by police from the chest of drawers also bore Group A bloodstains and, of eight coins selected from the Gladstone bag for testing, seven reacted positively to tests for blood and on the eighth was a small red spot that, when tested, was classified as 'human' blood.

Bertie Juggins was called to testify, as was Mr Rowley, who stated that all the while Griffin was at the Tontine Hotel he had not eaten so much as a bite of food. Mildred Edwards, a domestic help who worked at the hotel, confirmed that Griffin had eaten nothing and told the court that she had found the remains of an identity card in a drain and a medical card in the yard of the hotel. The medical card bore the name Griffin.

PC France was questioned and particular attention was paid to Griffin's collapse before signing his statement. France maintained that Griffin had been sober at the start of the interview, although obviously very nervous. 'Was it a nervous collapse or a drunken collapse?' enquired defence counsel Mr Foster.

'I would rather say a mixture of both,' replied France.

Griffin's defence counsel, Mr Long, told the court that his client had never denied that he was the man at the Queen's Head. Had this been part of the defence, then he would have had something to say about the circumstances under which Griffin's statements had been taken by the police. The defence weren't even denying that Griffin had killed Mrs Edge. Rather they maintained that Griffin had never had any prior intentions and his brain was so flooded with alcohol at the time that he was incapable of forming any. The robbery had been a moment of temptation and, rather than setting out to hurt Mrs Edge in order to steal from her, Griffin had not even touched her until the robbery had been affected and she had fought against him.

Frank Griffin was then summoned to the witness box, where he spent two hours and ten minutes, a period briefly interrupted by a power cut that suddenly plunged the court into semi-darkness.

Griffin first asked the court for their indulgence on account of his extreme nervousness then proceeded to relate his version of events of 6 September. Like John Edge, Griffin had worked at Sankey's, but had handed in his notice in favour of a more lucrative job at Sinclair's Works. On 4 September, he had visited Sankey's to collect his outstanding wages, but there had been a problem obtaining his 'cards', without which he could not start his new job.

Thus, according to Griffin, he had spent all day on both 4 and 5 September drinking at various public houses in the area and could recall very little of either afternoon or evening.

On 6 September, still unable to get his cards, he had intended to visit Sinclair's to tell them that he was unable to start work. He had called in at a number of pubs first and, passing the Queen's Head on his way to Sinclair's, had decided on impulse to stop there for yet another drink.

After two pints of beer, he tried to order a third, but Mrs Edge obviously believed that he had had more than enough to drink and offered to make him a cup of tea instead. She locked the front door and, at her suggestion, he had followed her to the private quarters at the back of the pub. As he went through the 'servery', he spotted the till and, again on impulse, decided to empty it.

He had removed a roll of banknotes and some loose change and also picked up a brown-paper container, which he put in his pocket. He was in the process of replacing the till drawer when Mrs Edge had come back and caught him red-handed.

She had shouted at him, 'What are you doing – robbing me?' and tried to snatch the till drawer from his hands. He had given her a shove and she had fallen heavily. Then she began to shout. He picked her up, putting his hand over her mouth to quieten her. She struggled and fell again. He helped her up and assisted her to her chair in the sitting room at the back of the pub. He cleaned up the blood from her face with a damp dishcloth and apologised to her before leaving, at which she had remarked sadly, 'The money won't do you any good, my lad.'

Claiming to have been drunk when he entered the pub, Griffin told the court that he could remember very little of what happened. He remembered waking up at the hostel then, a little later that evening, visiting the Plough Inn.

Having seen the police at the Apley Hostel on Friday, he learned for the first time that Mrs Edge had died and had left the hostel that afternoon, intending to visit his wife in Kidderminster to tell her that he was 'in trouble'.

When interviewed at the Tontine Hotel, he had been drinking steadily for several days and had not eaten any food and, as a result, had experienced a black out. Griffin maintained that he had never had any prior intention of robbing Mrs Edge, nor had he intended to hurt her in any way.

When cross-examined by Mr Foster for the prosecution, Griffin said that he had burned things at his room at Apley's Hostel simply because he was leaving and had too much to carry. He could offer no explanation for the bloodstained paper, coins or shirt other than that he had been present at the pub when Mrs Edge was injured – something he had never denied.

Griffin described the destruction of his identity and medical card as 'the foolish act of a drunken man trying to be clever'. He denied ever having told PC France that his name was Jenkins and insisted that he had taken only between £15 and £20 plus some silver from the pub – a far cry from the £85 that John Edge stated was missing.

Counsels for the defence and prosecution then gave their closing speeches. For the defence, Mr Long told the jury that, in order for Griffin to be found guilty of murder there must have been some intent on his part. Given the amount of alcohol consumed by Griffin prior to the death of Mrs Edge, the defence suggested that he was incapable of forming any such intent and therefore the correct verdict would be one of manslaughter.

Mr Foster, for the prosecution, reminded the jury of the number of witnesses, many of them publicans or policemen, who had testified about previous occasions when Griffin had had too much to drink. These included Bertie Juggins, the manager of the Apley Hostel, who had told the court that Griffin had only been moved to the room adjoining the manager's office after he had got very drunk two days before the murder and started behaving like a madman. Foster insisted that all the evidence pointed to Griffin being 'an aggressive and truculent man' who was frequently violent under the influence of alcohol.

It was left to the judge to sum up the case for the jury. Only two people knew for certain what had transpired in the Queen's Head on the afternoon of 6 September, he said, and one of those was now deceased. The other had told his story in court. Now, Mr Justice Cassels advised the jury to consider Professor Webster's testimony very carefully, although he didn't go quite as far as pointing out that Webster had stated that he would have expected a 'normal' person, who didn't have Mrs Edge's existing health problems, to have survived the injuries she received. Violent thieves, said Cassels, must take their victims as they find them and this particular victim just happened to have an enlarged heart.

Cassels told the jury that they should ask themselves whether or not they believed that Griffin had intended to cause any harm and, if they believed that he hadn't, then they must find him not guilty. They should also decide whether they believed that Griffin had drunk so much alcohol that he was incapable of forming the intent to kill or to cause grievous bodily harm. If this were the case then murder was not established and the accused could not be convicted.

Nevertheless, continued Cassels, there had been a killing, but if there had been no malice aforethought, in that there had been no prior intention, then the charge of murder should be reduced to one of manslaughter.

The jury retired, returning almost two hours later to ask the judge for more guidance on the state of mind necessary to separate murder and manslaughter, given the defendant's state of intoxication at the time of the killing. This was given and the jury retired again, returning after half an hour to pronounce Frank Griffin 'Guilty of the murder of Jane Edge'.

The judge awarded the mandatory sentence of death, which Griffin accepted without emotion, merely thanking his defence team for the 'superb fight' they had put up. The defence hadn't finished fighting and immediately filed an appeal, which was denied on 19 December. Consequently, on 4 January 1951, Frank Griffin became the last person to be hanged at Shrewsbury Gaol.

Almost sixty years later, reading accounts of the murder in the newspapers of the time raises some questions about the case in that some of the physical evidence found at the scene appears to support the account of Mrs Edge's death that Frank Griffin gave from the dock.

He stated that he had pushed Mrs Edge and that she had fallen in the bar and, although Professor Webster specifically stated that he didn't believe that Mrs Edge's injuries were consistent with a fall, blood and hairs from her head were found on the outer corner of a beer crate in the 'servery'. Griffin said that Mrs Edge's injuries occurred in the pub and that he had helped her to a chair in the back room, where he wiped her face with a dishcloth. In response to a question from the defence counsel, Professor Webster had agreed that 'there was nothing inconsistent with Mrs Edge having been helped from one place to another by some other person'. A dishcloth stained with Group A blood had been found near to the kitchen sink and a pool of blood was found in the bar, suggesting that Mrs Edge was first injured there.

The police recovered more than £150 in notes from the pub, most of it from upstairs. It seems inconceivable to imagine that a man who had visited premises with the specific intention of burgling it would have left so much cash untouched, unless he panicked and fled when he realised that Mrs Edge was injured. Admittedly, Griffin had been spending money a little more freely than usual in the aftermath of the murder and repaid several outstanding loans, but it must be remembered that on the day before he had collected his final wage packet from Sankey's, the contents of which amounted to almost £7. He also purported to have about £20 of savings.

Finally, there is the question of the validity of any of Frank Griffin's statements, given that he was almost certainly extremely drunk when first questioned. Even discounting his allegation that he was bought two half-bottles of gin by the police on the journey to Wellington police station, there is the testimony of Mr Rowley, who stated in court that Griffin was perfectly sober when the police entered his room at the Tontine Hotel and yet, two hours later, he left the room in a state of collapse, having apparently eaten nothing for at least twenty-four hours and consumed two half-bottles of gin, plus additional measures of scotch. Several witnesses had testified in court that Frank Griffin's normal drink of choice was beer and that he didn't usually drink spirits in excess. On 11 September, Dr L.R.G. Glanville, a doctor from London who was then serving as a locum doctor in Wellington, examined Griffin at Wellington police station. Glanville had then found him to be suffering from 'post-alcoholic depression' and had prescribed three fingers of gin as a 'pick me up'.

That Frank Griffin was involved in the violent death of Jane Edge seems indisputable – whether the correct charge was murder or manslaughter is open to debate.

[Note: Mrs Edge's son is alternatively named as both John and Jack Edge in contemporary newspaper reports of the case.]

27

'I'LL SEARCH FOR HER, IF IT TAKES ALL NIGHT'

Near Atcham, 1953

Atcham Camp was seen as a safe place to bring up children. Many of the people living and working there had young families and the children were always playing together, in and out of each other's houses, rarely far from adult supervision. However, in 1953, the perception of the camp changed when a little girl went out to visit a neighbour and never came home.

Twelve-year-old Betty Selina Smith was a friendly and outgoing, yet sensible, girl who spent the early part of the evening of 21 July 1953 at a social event organised by her school. When she came home, she told her mother that she was going to see neighbours Mr and Mrs Hooper to collect some magazines that they had promised to give her. Dorothy Smith had no objections – the Hoopers were a respectable, well-liked family and Betty often played with their children.

When Betty arrived at the Hooper's house, she spent an hour or so playing dominoes with seven-year-old Keith Hooper. As Keith's bedtime approached, Betty collected her magazines and prepared to go home.

Meanwhile, Betty's mother had been dozing and, when she woke up, she realised that Betty had not yet come home. She immediately cycled the short distance to the Hooper's house to find her.

When she got there, Mrs Hooper was alone with her children. Her husband, Desmond, had gone out, leaving her a note saying that he had gone to look for some pigeons. Mrs Hooper, who had been out herself earlier that evening, had not seen Betty at all, but suggested that her husband may have seen her. The two women sat down to await his return.

He arrived home at 1.45 a.m., in a somewhat dishevelled state. He was wet and muddy, perspiring heavily and was also not wearing his tie, which was quite unusual back in the 1950s. Expressing his distress at hearing that Betty was missing, he told her worried mother that he had sent her home with her magazines when he had to go out. 'I'll search for her, if it takes all night,' he offered, while Mrs Hooper suggested that Mrs Smith telephone the police and report the child missing. However, Mrs Smith was unwilling to cause a fuss and it was only after a night of searching for the missing child had proved fruitless that the police were called.

They immediately launched a search of the area, as well as questioning people on the camp who might be able to throw some light on Betty's disappearance. Naturally, they started their questions with the person who was known to have seen her last – Desmond Donald Hooper.

Hooper was a keen pigeon fancier and, although he didn't have any birds of his own, he frequently helped with those owned by Richard Harris of nearby Attingham Home Farm. Hooper told the police that, on the night of Betty's disappearance, he had been to the farm to search for some lost pigeons. He had spent approximately an hour and a half trying to retrieve the pigeons, which had roosted high in the rafters of a barn but, as he had no ladder, he had been unable to reach them and had returned home. Hooper insisted that he had sent Betty

Atcham. (© N. Sly, 2008)

home at about 10.40 p.m. and, when he last saw her, she was running towards her house on Deer Park. When the police spoke to his son, Keith, the child seemed to corroborate his father's story, saying that he had heard him saying goodnight to Betty at around that time.

Apparently, very few people had been out and about on the camp at that hour, since the police received no further information, nor any sightings of Betty. Their search of the camp revealed no clues as to the whereabouts of the missing child and it was therefore decided to expand the search area. On 24 July, a blue pinstriped jacket was found lying on the ground next to an airshaft, which ventilated a tunnel in the disused Shropshire Union Canal between Uffington and Berwick Wharf.

When the police investigated the 44ft-deep shaft, they found the body of Betty Smith at the bottom, lying in several feet of water, a man's tie wrapped tightly round her neck. A later post-mortem examination revealed that the child had been partially strangled with the tie, but had still been alive when she was thrown head first into the airshaft. Marks on her body indicated that she had been firmly held down by somebody, but Betty was fully clothed and there was no evidence to suggest that she had been raped or even sexually assaulted. The time of her death was judged to have been at around midnight on 21/22 July.

The police concentrated their enquiries on locating the owner of the jacket found abandoned at the top of the airshaft, appealing in local and national newspapers for the assistance of the public. A motorist came forward to say that he had seen a man and a girl walking in the vicinity of the airshaft on the night of the murder. The child had been wearing an adult's jacket, but, since she had not seemed to be in any distress, the motorist had thought no more about it until he read the appeals in the newspapers.

Desmond Hooper denied ownership of the jacket, but his brother, Bernard, contacted the police to say that it closely resembled one that he had sold to his brother two years earlier. A local tailor, George Herbert Lee, confirmed his statement, saying that he recognised a repair that he had made to the jacket.

However, there were doubtless many men in the area who owned similar jackets and Hooper insisted that the jacket he had brought from his brother had been long since passed on to his father-in-law and had now been made into a rag rug. Hence the police focused on checking his story of having spent the night of the murder looking for pigeons at Attingham Home Farm and, unfortunately for Hooper, his alibi was unsubstantiated.

The police interviewed farmer Richard Harris, who told them that he had neither seen nor heard Hooper at the farm on the night in question. Furthermore, he found it impossible to believe that anyone had visited the farm without him noticing, as his dogs generally barked very loudly whenever someone entered the yard. Another resident of the farm, Mrs Lewis, occupied a bedroom that looked out onto the farmyard and the barn where Cooper said he had been trying to catch the birds. She too told the police that the dogs hadn't made any noise and that she had not seen Hooper that night.

Hooper was arrested and charged with the murder of Betty Selina Smith and remanded in custody to await the commencement of legal proceedings against him. Meanwhile, the police continued their investigations and, by late August 1953, Hooper's solicitor, Mr David Harris, had had enough of waiting for them to conclude and made a formal complaint against the Director of Public Prosecutions.

Harris accepted that Hooper could not be given bail while the police investigations were ongoing, but was considering making an application to a Judge of the High Court to either bring the case forward or to release Hooper, who was, according to Harris, very anxious. Hooper was intending to plead 'Not Guilty' to the charge of murder against him and, said his solicitor, it was therefore possible that an innocent man was being kept in custody and that his physical and mental health could be permanently affected as a result.

Despite Mr Harris's protests, at his sixth appearance before magistrates, Hooper was again remanded in custody for another week. The Deputy Chief Constable of Shropshire, Mr John McKiernan, stated that there were still more enquiries to be made and it was therefore with the full support of the DPP that he was asking for a further remand.

In the event, Cooper had to stay on remand in prison for some time, as it wasn't until 1 October that he was finally committed for trial at the Shropshire Assizes. News of his committal came with a statement that, while he had been remanded in custody, a fellow prisoner, Frank Baker, had approached prison staff saying that Hooper had told him 'I did it'. However, the prosecution stated that they regarded Baker's information as a complete fabrication and did not intend to call him as a witness at the trial.

The proceedings opened on 23 November under Mr Justice Cassels. Mr E. Ryder Richardson and Paul Wrightson prosecuted, while G.G. Baker and Peter Northcote represented Hooper who, as expected, pleaded 'Not Guilty'.

Using aerial photographs of the area – apparently for the first time ever in a British court – the prosecution outlined what they believed had happened on the night of the murder. Mr Ryder Richardson QC alleged that Betty had left Hooper's house with Hooper at about nine o'clock on the evening of 21 July, wearing the pinstriped jacket over her own clothes against the evening chill. The couple had walked together for several miles before Hooper came to the airshaft and threw the child down it, after first trying to strangle her with his tie.

In his defence, Hooper tried to suggest that the murder was committed by a friend of his, a seventeen-year-old store man who also worked at the camp. According to Hooper, Clive Albert Lloyd had a grudge against Betty and had sworn to get even with her because she had once hit his sister, Maureen.

Lloyd was questioned intensely in court and denied all of the allegations that Hooper had made against him. 'You did not like Betty Smith, did you?' asked the counsel for the defence.

'I saw nothing wrong with the girl,' replied Lloyd.

Lloyd told the court that Hooper had once lent him a jacket similar to 'exhibit seven', the jacket that had been found at the top of the airshaft, but that he had subsequently returned it. (The jacket was, in fact, proving to be a rather contentious piece of evidence since Hooper's brother, who had previously been so certain that it was the jacket he had sold, now stated in court that he had doubts.)

Denying that he had arranged to meet Hooper on the night of the murder to look for pigeons, Lloyd admitted that he had been for a cycle ride with the accused at the beginning of June, during which they had stopped to look at the canal. He also denied telling Hooper on that occasion that the canal would be a good place to hide a dead body.

Although Lloyd stated that he had no reason to dislike Hooper and had always considered him a friend, it emerged in court that Mrs Hooper had made a complaint to the police that, after her husband's arrest, Lloyd had suggested to her that she should have sexual intercourse with him. Although Lloyd denied this allegation too, he admitted that the police had warned him about his conduct and told him to stay away from Mrs Hooper in future.

On the night of the murder, Lloyd told the court that he had arrived home at 9.30 p.m. and had not left the house again. After Lloyd had finished his testimony, an application was made to the judge by the defence counsel to prohibit him from going home that evening, as his family were due to be called as witnesses the following day. The judge agreed that Lloyd should not have the opportunity to discuss the case with other potential witnesses and arranged an overnight place in a hostel for him.

As the trial continued, the thoroughness of the police investigation into the case showed why Hooper had been remanded in custody for so long prior to his trial. Every attempt made by Hooper's defence counsel to exonerate him was countered by the findings of the police. It even emerged that seven-year-old Keith Hooper, who had said that he had heard his father bidding goodnight to Betty, had previously been carefully coached by his father in what to say.

Thus, in spite of the fact that the police had never been able to prove conclusively that the jacket and the tie used to strangle Betty belonged to Hooper and despite the lack of any apparent motive for the child's murder, the jury found him 'Guilty' and he was sentenced to death.

The defence immediately appealed the case, but the appeal was denied and, on 20 January 1954, Albert Pierrepoint, assisted by Robert Stewart, hanged Hooper at Shrewsbury Prison. The residents of Atcham at the time felt almost as one that he died too easily.

28

'STEP ONE, YOU FIND A GIRL TO LOVE ...'

American singer Eddie Cochran had several chart hits in England in the late 1950s, including *Summertime Blues*, *C'mon, Everybody* and *Three Steps to Heaven*. It was while he was touring in the UK in April 1960 that Cochran was tragically killed in a car crash near Chippenham, Wiltshire.

Barry Charles Smallman of St Nicholas' Crescent, Bridgnorth, dreamed of becoming a rock star just like his idol Cochran. During the day, Smallman worked as a labourer on building sites, but after work, he and the rock and roll group he fronted would head to the bright lights of Wolverhampton, where they were a popular live act in the pubs and clubs.

At nineteen, Smallman was an awkward youth who was seen by some to be a bit of a mother's boy. Extremely handsome, with an engaging grin, he liked girls, but, unless he had a few drinks for Dutch courage, was always rather uncomfortable in their company. According to his mother, Barry was a good boy who preferred playing darts and dominoes at the pub to chasing girls, but after drinking he would do anything for a dare.

Barry's father had been killed during the Second World War, leaving his mother to bring up Barry and his five brothers alone. Little wonder that she was rather overprotective, particularly as Barry began to develop a devoted following among the local girls, who found his on-stage persona exciting and rather glamorous. Letters were put through the door of his home, which Barry's mother promptly destroyed before he could read them, apparently at his request. Girls who called at the house were told that Barry was not in and, when Barry somehow found himself engaged, his mother went straight to his fiancée's parents and got the

A postcard of Bridgnorth High Street, 1950s. (Author's collection)

engagement broken off, just three days after the girl tried to persuade Barry to leave home.

Mrs Smallman's opinion of Jean Harrison is not recorded. Having left school at fifteen, Jean had continued to live with her parents in Broseley for two years before moving to the Grove Estate in Bridgnorth, where she lodged with her aunt and uncle, Mr and Mrs Groves. Jean was apparently something of a 'wild child', who liked nothing better than attending dances in Wolverhampton with her girlfriends. She was allowed to date boys, but her aunt and uncle only permitted her to bring them home on Sundays and kept a strict eye on her to make sure that she behaved herself.

Jean moved in with her aunt and uncle in August 1960, but by September of that year, she had already all but abandoned the nightlife of Wolverhampton in favour of 'going steady'. Her new boyfriend was the charismatic, yet strangely shy, Barry Smallman, who lived close to her aunt's home. Now, when Barry sang love songs with his group, the words were directed to just one girl in the crowd of fans. However, the fact that Barry had a steady girlfriend didn't seem to deter his multitude of teenage admirers from making a play for him, a situation that seemed to embarrass Barry and certainly made Jean jealous. Yet, when Jean wasn't around, Barry was not above encouraging his young fans and apparently leading them to believe that he might just be available.

Jean eventually plucked up the courage to introduce her boyfriend to her aunt who, much to Jean's astonishment, took an instant liking to the young man and began to give the girl a little more freedom than she had in the past. The curfew that had previously been so strictly enforced was relaxed and Barry was trusted to take care of Jean and to make sure that she got home safely. No doubt the girl's aunt would have been horrified to know that her niece and the pleasant young man were regularly having sexual intercourse in nearby Grove Woods.

On 19 October 1960, Jean finished a late shift at the carpet factory where she worked and arrived back at her aunt's house at 10.15 p.m. Telling her aunt that she was going to meet Barry, she left to go to the Fox Hotel in Wolverhampton, where Barry and his group had been booked to provide the music for a dance. On this occasion, Barry did not get Jean safely home and when she was still out at 1.50 a.m., her aunt called the police and reported her missing.

Knowing that Jean had intended to meet Barry in Wolverhampton, the police took Mrs Groves round to the Smallman's house at 2 a.m. Mrs Smallman told them that Barry was asleep in bed, but agreed to wake him and ask him if he knew Jean's whereabouts. Barry told them that he hadn't seen Jean at all that night.

The police felt that it was a little early to worry about Jean, no doubt assuming that she had most probably spent the night with a friend and would return in the morning. Her aunt spent a sleepless night and, when Jean still hadn't come back at 8.30 a.m., she set off to talk to as many of Jean's friends whose names she could recall. She soon learned that Jean had been seen leaving the Fox Hotel in Wolverhampton with Barry and went straight to Bridgnorth police station to inform the police of her findings.

Officers immediately went to the building site in Dawley, where Barry was working that day, to question him about Jean. After initially denying that he knew anything about her, he eventually burst into tears and told police that he had taken her to Grove Wood, where the couple had made love. However, he swore that he had left her alive and well to make her own way home.

Jean should have clocked on at the carpet factory at 2 p.m. that afternoon and, when she didn't arrive at work, the police called in dog handlers and began a search of Grove Wood. It took just ten minutes before the dogs found the body of a young girl, lying on her back in the undergrowth. Her blouse was open and her bra had been pulled down beneath her breasts, which showed clear and unmistakeable bite marks, as did her neck. Her discarded knickers lay several feet from her body.

A post-mortem examination conducted by Home Office pathologist Dr Gerald Evans determined that Jean had been manually strangled after having sexual intercourse. There were no signs that she had been raped and every indication that, not only had the intercourse been consensual, but also that Jean had been sexually active for some time.

Witnesses came forward to say that, on the previous evening, they had seen Jean and Barry walking hand-in-hand up the steps that led into Grove Wood. Barry was arrested and charged with Jean's murder, appearing before magistrates at Bridgnorth in November 1960, where he pleaded 'Not Guilty'. He was committed for trial at the next Shropshire Assizes.

His trial opened before Mr Justice Barry on 25 November 1960, by which time Barry Smallman had decided to plead 'Guilty' to the charge against him. Thus, his trial lasted only five minutes.

Only three years earlier, the British government had made the first step towards the eventual abolition of capital punishment by passing the 1957 Homicide Act. From March of that year, only those acts designated as 'Capital Murder' were deemed punishable by execution – murder committed in the course or furtherance of theft, murder by shooting or explosion, murder whilst resisting arrest or during an escape, murder of a police or prison officer or two murders committed on different occasions. The murder of Jean Harrison didn't fit into any of these categories, so Mr Justice Barry passed the now mandatory sentence, which was life imprisonment.

It was generally accepted that, in killing his girlfriend, Barry Smallman had acted in a way that was completely out of character. Much was made of the apparent deterioration in Jean's behaviour after her move to Bridgnorth. Even the prosecuting counsel at the trial, Mr John Wood, pointed out to the jury that Jean Harrison had been no angel, was sexually active and had been seen drunk more than once. It was believed that Barry had been drinking heavily at the time of the murder and that, while they were engaged in having intercourse, Jean had taunted him, almost daring him to strangle her. 'If he had been allowed to come straight home, nothing like this would have happened,' said his mother, in an interview with the local paper after the trial.

Barry Smallman was eventually released from prison on licence in 1967, having served just seven years of his life sentence.

'I AM SIGNING MY DEATH WARRANT, AREN'T I?'

Shrewsbury, 1960

Like many twenty-one-year-old men, George Riley lived for the weekends. Friday was payday and, with money in his pocket, weekends were the time for indulging in his favourite pastimes – drinking, dancing and meeting girls.

Yet, even though he liked a good time, George was quite a sensible young man and wasn't completely feckless with his money. On Friday 7 October 1960, having picked up his wages from his job as a trainee butcher, George purchased some savings stamps on his way back to his family home in Westlands Road, Shrewsbury. Having given the stamps to his mother for safekeeping, George also handed her some money for his 'board and lodgings'. Then, with his financial obligations met, the remainder of his wage packet was his to spend as he wished.

George ate tea with his mother, father and brother, Terry, and then got dressed for a night out on the town. At 7.15 p.m., his friend, Tony Brown, called for him in his car and the two men went to the first of the several pubs they were to visit that night while they decided which of the local dances to attend.

They eventually plumped for the dance at the Sentinel Works at Harlescott, but were in no hurry to get there, visiting a few more public houses on the way. By the time they reached the dance, George Riley was well on his way to being intoxicated and, once there, he drank even more alcohol. At some point in the evening, he lost count of the number of drinks he had actually consumed, but was later to estimate that he had drunk at least eight or nine pints of beer and eight whiskies with orange. However many drinks he had, it was certainly more alcohol

Westlands Road, Shrewsbury. (© N. Sly, 2008)

than he had ever imbibed at one sitting in his life before. Even so, many people at the dance – including two policemen – would later say that although he was lively and noisy, he was exuberant rather than drunk.

George and Tony had not been at the dance long when an argument broke out between George and a friend, Laurence 'Lol' Griffiths. It ended with the two men wrestling together rather ineffectually on the floor, both having consumed too much alcohol to be sufficiently coordinated to put up a proper fight. They were eventually pulled apart by a policeman, PC Reginald Mason, who advised Riley to go home.

Riley and Tony Brown left the dance in Brown's car in the early hours of the morning of Saturday 8 October. They gave another man a lift home, dropping him off before pulling up outside Riley's house at 1.30 a.m. The house was in darkness, the rest of the Riley family having long since retired to bed, but unfortunately George discovered at this point that he had left his house key in the pocket of his other suit. Not wanting to disturb his family, he slipped into the garage and sat down on an old sofa that was stored there. George was later to claim that he went straight to sleep.

A little further along Westlands Road from the Riley's home lived a sixty-two-year-old widow, Mrs Adeline Mary Smith. Her sister, Miss Olive Martin, had visited her earlier that evening and the two women had made arrangements to go out together the next day.

Olive Martin telephoned her sister early on Saturday morning to discuss these arrangements, but nobody answered the telephone. Somewhat concerned, Olive walked to her sister's house, arriving at about ten o'clock. She was disturbed to see that all the curtains were still drawn across and became even more worried when her knocking on the door brought no response from inside the house.

Olive Martin went to her sister's neighbour for assistance. Army sergeant Brian Bean went round to the back of the house, noticing as he did that a pane of glass in the French window had been broken. He slipped his hand through the broken window and undid the latch and, walking through the house to the front door, he opened it to let Olive in. Olive quickly checked upstairs and it was she who found her sister lying dead in a large pool of blood on her bedroom floor. Her nightdress was ripped to shreds and she had obviously been beaten to death, since her face was almost unrecognisable. Some of her teeth had been knocked out and it was evident from the marks on her head and face that whoever had beaten her had used his fists and that her attacker had been wearing a ring.

The police were called and immediately began house-to-house enquiries. Neighbour Phyllis Kay told them that she had heard a single scream at about two o'clock that morning. As the police progressed further along Westlands Road, they called at the Riley's home where they were very interested to note that George Riley had several fresh scratches on his face.

Questioned about the scratches, Riley told officers about his evening of drinking, claiming he had received the marks on his face during his fight with Lol Griffiths. He explained that he had come home in the early hours of the morning and, having forgotten his key, had slept in the garage until five o'clock, when he had noticed a light shining from the dining room of his parent's house. He had tapped on the window and been let into the house by his brother, Terry. However, when police asked to see the clothes he had been wearing the previous night, they found his shoes, socks and the cuffs of his trousers covered in mud. There was even a live slug still attached to the mud on his clothes.

Riley told the police that the mud had come from his driveway, which had recently been flooded. Yet while searching Mrs Smith's house and garden, the police had found footprints in the soft, muddy earth next to a stile that led from Mrs Smith's garden into the fields beyond.

The police officers questioning Riley decided to gamble and told him they believed that he was responsible for the murder of Mrs Smith. They assured him that they had found sufficient evidence at her house to prove his involvement, telling him about the footprints and also saying that they had found fingerprints at the scene of the crime. Riley obviously believed them.

Now he told the police that he had been in Mrs Smith's house before and was aware that she usually kept her purse in her handbag in her bedroom. When he arrived home the previous evening, he realised that he had spent far too much money on drink, leaving himself just a few coppers to last until his next payday. In his drunken, befuddled state, it had seemed like a good idea to rob Mrs Smith.

Having broken a windowpane at the back of her house, he had gone to Mrs Smith's bedroom in search of her handbag. However, Mrs Smith had woken up and jumped out of bed, intent on protecting her property. Riley had struck her hard on her face, at which she fell to the floor, where he knelt over her and punched her repeatedly in the face until she lost consciousness. He insisted that Mrs Smith had not been dead when he left her house and that his only intention had been to rob her. Having beaten the elderly lady senseless, he had become frightened and had left without taking any money. Once outside, he had heard footsteps in the street, so had climbed the stile at the end of Mrs Smith's garden and walked across the fields to the Grapes Inn at Bicton. From there, he had made his way home by road.

George Riley was arrested and charged with the murder of Mrs Adeline Mary Smith and, while in custody at the police station, he wrote out a statement confessing to killing the elderly woman. Since the 1957 Homicide Act was passed in England, capital punishment for murder had been all but abolished. However, it still remained the prescribed punishment for just a handful of types of murder, one of these being 'Murder in the course or furtherance of theft.'

Since Riley admitted that his sole intention had been to steal from Mrs Smith, her murder was punishable by execution, should he be convicted. This fact had not escaped George Riley's notice and, as he signed his statement, he observed wryly, 'I am signing my death warrant, aren't I?'

Riley was committed to appear at the next Shropshire Assizes. His trial opened on 7 December 1960 at Stafford, since it was believed that Riley stood little chance of finding a neutral jury in his hometown of Shrewsbury, where the trial would normally have been held and where the public opinion was very much against him. Mr Justice Barry presided and Kenneth Mynett prosecuted, with E. Ryder Richardson and Peter Northcote defending.

Apart from Riley's confession, there was very little other than circumstantial evidence against him. His only real defence was that he was so drunk at the time of the murder that he was not in control of himself when he killed Mrs Smith. However, several people who had seen him at the dance before Mrs Smith's murder claimed in court that he was 'lively' rather than drunk and his friend Tony Brown, who had given him a lift home, told the court that, when he left him, Riley was able to stand and walk unaided and was not slurring his words.

The police believed that Mrs Smith had made the fresh scratches on Riley's face, as she bravely tried to fight him off. Riley maintained that he had received them in his fight with Lol Smith, but PC Mason, the policeman who had separated the two men, testified that Riley's face had not been injured in any way in the scuffle.

The defence claimed that the statement given by Riley when first questioned by the police was inadmissible, since he had not been properly cautioned. Yet it was Riley's confession that most influenced the jury, even though he had later retracted it. Seemingly unable to ignore the confession, the jury returned a verdict of 'Guilty' and, because of Riley's admission of his intent to steal from his victim,

A postcard of Shrewsbury High Street, 1940s. (Author's collection)

which made the murder a capital offence, Mr Justice Barry sentenced him to death by judicial hanging.

An appeal was immediately lodged, but was later disallowed. Nevertheless, those connected with the case found it difficult to believe that Riley would actually hang and, on the eve of his execution, even his fellow prisoners made their protests known, setting small fires and banging metal objects, making a terrible din.

Yet the anticipated reprieve never came and, on Thursday 9 February, executioner Harry Allen ensured that George Riley earned the dubious distinction of being the last person ever to be hanged at Shrewsbury Prison.

Tragically, Mrs Adeline Mary Smith, who was known as a kind and generous woman, had only 3s 7½d halfpenny in her purse when she met her violent death at the hands of George Riley.

BIBLIOGRAPHY
& REFERENCES

BOOKS

Eddleston, John J., *The Encyclopaedia of Executions*, London, John Blake, 2004
Glover, George, *Shropshire Murders*, Kington, Arch, 1992
Harrison, Paul, *Shropshire Murder Casebook*, Newbury, Countryside Books, 1994
Hunt, Anthony, *Murder in Mind*, Warwick, QuercuS [*sic*], 2005

NEWSPAPERS

Shrewsbury News
Shrewsbury Chronicle
The Times
Wellington Journal

Certain websites have also been consulted in the compilation of this book, but since they have a habit of disappearing, to avoid frustration, they have not been cited.

INDEX